Warnings to the Churches

Warnings to the Churches

2 M'Cheyne

10 Novice meets heretic

6 Jewel : Peace with God, not men

TO HELP OTHERS

_____ Cheque/PO/Cash/Visa/Access

Expiry Date _____

ARRON, ROSS-SHIRE IV54 8YD

e by Deed of Covenant. Please consider using
or more. Please write for Details.

Warnings to the Churches

J. C. RYLE

THE BANNER OF TRUTH TRUST

THE BANNER OF TRUTH TRUST
3 Murrayfield Road, Edinburgh EH 12 6EL
P.O. Box 621, Carlisle, Pennsylvania 17013, USA

*

This selection first published 1967
Reprinted 1992
ISBN 0 85151 043 4

*

Printed and bound in Great Britain by
BPCC Hazells Ltd
Aylesbury, Bucks, England
Member of BPCC Ltd

Contents

TWO OF THE EARLIEST PAPERBACK TITLES PUB-
lished by the Trust were J. C. Ryle's *Five English Reformers* and *Five Christian Leaders*, which have both
proved extremely popular. The present volume contains
addresses and articles by Ryle which have long been out
of print. Most of these first appeared in *Home Truths*, col-
lections of Ryle's addresses, several series of which were
published. The five closing chapters of *Warnings to the
Churches* were also included in *Knots Untied* (first published in 1877). This last work has often been reprinted,
but in an abridged form omitting these chapters. They are
included, however, in the 1964 James Clarke reprint.

The eight papers making up this edition of *Warnings to
the Churches* have never previously been published
together as a unit, to the present publishers' knowledge.
They are ideally suited for this purpose, however, present-
ing in concise form Ryle's prophetic message to the
Churches in his own day, and in ours.

1 : The True Church*

'Upon this rock I will build my Church, and the gates of hell shall not prevail against it' (Matt. 16 : 18).

WE LIVE IN A WORLD IN WHICH ALL THINGS ARE passing away. Kingdoms, empires, cities, ancient institutions, families, all are liable to change and corruption. One universal law seems to prevail everywhere. In all created things there is a tendency to decay.

There is something saddening and depressing in this. What profit hath a man in the labour of his hands? Is there nothing that shall stand? Is there nothing that shall last? Is there nothing that shall endure? Is there nothing of which we can say – This shall continue for evermore? You have the answer to these questions in the words of our text. Our Lord Jesus Christ speaks of something which shall continue, and not pass away. There is one created thing which is an exception to the universal rule to which I have referred. There is one thing which shall never perish and pass away. That thing is the building founded upon the rock – the Church of our Lord Jesus Christ. He declares, in the words you have heard to-night: 'Upon this rock I will build My Church, and the gates of hell shall not prevail against it.'

There are five things in these words which demand your attention :–

I. – *You have a Building:* 'My Church.'

II. – *A Builder:* Christ says, 'I will build My Church.'

* The following Sermon was preached at Weston-super-Mare, in August, 1858, on the occasion of the Aggregate Clerical Meeting, held there under the presidency of Archdeacon Law.

III. – *A Foundation:* 'Upon this rock I will build My Church.'

IV. – *Perils Implied:* 'The gates of hell.'

V. – *Security Asserted.* – 'The gates of hell shall not prevail against it.'

May God bless the words that shall be spoken. May we all search our own hearts to-night, and know whether or not we belong to this one Church. May we all go home to reflect and to pray!

I. – You have, firstly, a *Building* mentioned in the text. The Lord Jesus Christ speaks of 'My Church.'

Now what is this Church? Few inquiries can be made of more importance than this. For want of due attention to this subject, the errors that have crept into the Church, and into the world, are neither few nor small.

The Church of our text is no material building. It is no temple made with hands, of wood, or brick, or stone, or marble. It is a company of men and women. It is no particular visible Church on earth. It is not the Eastern Church or the Western Church. It is not the Church of England, or the Church of Scotland; – much less is it the Church of Rome. The Church of our text is one that makes far less show in the eyes of man, but is of far more importance in the eyes of God.

The Church of our text is made up of all true believers in the Lord Jesus Christ. It comprehends all who have repented of sin, and fled to Christ by faith, and been made new creatures in Him. It comprises all God's elect, all who have received God's grace, all who have been washed in Christ's blood, all who have been clothed in Christ's righteousness, all who have been born again and sanctified by Christ's Spirit. All such, of every nation, and people, and tongue, compose the Church of our text. This is the body of Christ. This is the flock of Christ. This is the bride. This is the Lamb's wife. This is 'the holy Catholic Church' of the Apostles' Creed. This is the 'blessed company of all faithful people,' spoken of in the Communion Service of our Prayer-book. This is the Church on the rock.

The members of this Church do not all worship God in the same way, or use the same form of government. Our own 34th Article declares, 'It is not necessary that ceremonies should be in all places one and alike.' But they all worship with one heart. They are all led by one Spirit. They are all really and truly holy. They can all say 'Alleluia,' and they can all reply 'Amen.'

This is that Church, to which all visible Churches on earth are servants and handmaidens. Whether they are Episcopalian, Independent, or Presbyterian, they all serve the interests of the one true Church. They are the scaffolding, behind which the great building is carried on. They are the husk, under which the living kernel grows. They have their various degrees of usefulness. The best and worthiest of them is that which trains up most members for Christ's true Church. But no visible Church has any right to say, 'We are the only true Church. We are the men, and wisdom shall die with us.' No visible Church should ever dare to say, 'We shall stand for ever. The gates of hell shall not prevail against me.'

This is that Church to which belong the Lord's precious promises of preservation, continuance, protection, and final glory. 'Whatsoever,' says Hooker, 'we read in Scripture, concerning the endless love and saving mercy which God showeth towards His Churches, the only proper subject thereof is this Church, which we properly term the mystical body of Christ.' Small and despised as the true Church may be in this world, it is precious and honourable in the sight of God. The temple of Solomon in all its glory was mean and contemptible, in comparison with that Church which is built upon a rock.

Men and brethren, see that you hold sound doctrine upon the subject of 'the Church.' A mistake here may lead on to dangerous and soul-ruining errors. The Church which is made up of true believers, is the Church for which we, who are ministers, are specially ordained to preach. The Church which comprises all who repent and believe the Gospel, is the Church to which we desire you to belong. Our work is not done, and our hearts are not satisfied, until you are made new creatures, and are members of the one true Church. Outside of this Church there can be no salvation.

II. – I pass on to the second point, to which I proposed to call your attention. Our text contains not merely a building, but a *Builder*. The Lord Jesus Christ declares, '*I* will build My Church.'

The true Church of Christ is tenderly cared for by all the three persons of the blessed Trinity. In the economy of redemption, beyond all doubt, God the Father chooses, and God the Holy Ghost sanctifies, every member of Christ's mystical body. God the Father, God the Son, and God the Holy Ghost, three Persons and one God, co-operate for the salvation of every saved soul. This is truth, which ought never to be forgotten. Nevertheless, there is a peculiar sense in which the help of the Church is laid on the Lord Jesus Christ. He is peculiarly and pre-eminently the Redeemer and the Saviour. Therefore it is, that we find

Him saying in our text, 'I will build: the work of building is my special work.'

It is Christ who calls the members of the Church in due time. They are 'the called of Jesus Christ.' (Rom. 1:6.) It is Christ who quickens them. 'The Son quickeneth whom He will.' (John 5:21.) It is Christ who washes away their sins. He 'has loved us, and washed us from our sins in His own blood.' (Rev. 1:5.) It is Christ who gives them peace. 'Peace I leave with you, My peace I give unto you.' (John 14:27). It is Christ who gives them eternal life. 'I give unto them eternal life, and they shall never perish.' (John 10:28). It is Christ who grants them repentance. 'Him hath God exalted to be a Prince and a Saviour to give repentance.' (Acts 5:31.) It is Christ who enables them to become God's children. 'To as many as received Him, to them gave He power to become the sons of God.' (John 1:12.) It is Christ who carries on the work within them when it is begun. 'Because I live, ye shall live also.' (John 14:19.) In short, it has 'pleased the Father that in Christ should all fulness dwell.' (Col. 1:19.) He is the author and finisher of faith. From Him every joint and member of the mystical body of Christians is supplied. Through Him they are strengthened for duty. By Him they are kept from falling. He shall preserve them to the end, and present them faultless before the Father's throne with exceeding great joy. He is all things, and all in all to believers.

The mighty agent by whom the Lord Jesus Christ carries out this work in the number of His Churches, is, without doubt, the Holy Ghost. He it is who applies Christ and His benefits to the soul. He it is who is ever renewing, awakening, convincing, leading to the cross, transforming, taking out of the world, stone after stone, and adding it to the mystical building.

But the great Chief Builder, who has undertaken to execute the work of redemption and bring it to completion, is the Son of God: the Word who was made flesh. It is Jesus Christ who 'builds.'

In building the true Church, the Lord Jesus condescends to use many subordinate instruments. The ministry of the Gospel, the circulation of the Scriptures, the friendly rebuke, the word spoken in season, the drawing influence of afflictions – all, all are means and appliances by which His work is carried on. But Christ is the great superintending architect, ordering, guiding, directing all that is done. What the sun is to the whole solar system, that Christ is to all the members of the true Church. 'Paul may plant, and Apollos water, but God giveth the increase.' Ministers may preach, and writers may write, but the Lord Jesus Christ alone can build. And except He builds, the work stands still.

Great is the wisdom wherewith the Lord Jesus Christ builds His Church. All is done at the right time, and in the right way. Each stone in its turn is put in the right place. Sometimes He chooses great stones, and sometimes He chooses small stones. Sometimes the work goes on fast, and sometimes it goes on slowly. Man is frequently impatient, and thinks that nothing is doing. But man's time is not God's time. A thousand years in His sight are but as a single day. The great Builder makes no mistakes. He knows what He is doing. He sees the end from the beginning. He works by a perfect, unalterable and certain plan. The mightiest conceptions of architects, like Michael Angelo and Wren, are mere trifling child's play, in comparison with Christ's wise counsels respecting His Church.

Great is the condescension and mercy, which Christ exhibits in building His Church. He often chooses the most

unlikely and roughest stones, and fits them into a most excellent work. He despises none, and rejects none, on
account of former sins and past transgressions. He delights
to show mercy. He often takes the most thoughtless and
ungodly, and transforms them into polished corners of His
spiritual temple.

Great is the power which Christ displays in building
His Church. He carries on his work in spite of opposition
from the world, the flesh, and the devil. In storm, in tem-
pest, through troublous times, silently, quietly, without
noise, without stir, without excitement, the building pro-
gresses, like Solomon's temple. 'I will work,' He declares,
'and none shall let it.'

Brethren, the children of this world take little or no interest in the building of this Church. They care little for
the conversion of souls. What are broken spirits and peni-
tent hearts to them? It is all foolishness in their eyes. But
while the children of this world care nothing, there is joy
in the presence of the angels of God. For the preserving of
that Church, the laws of nature have oftentimes been sus-
pended. For the good of that Church, all the providential
dealings of God in this world are ordered and arranged.
For the elect's sake, wars are brought to an end, and peace
is given to a nation. Statesmen, rulers, emperors, kings,
presidents, heads of governments, have their schemes and
plans, and think them of vast importance. But there is
another work going on of infinitely greater moment, for
which they are all but as the axes and saws in God's hands.
That work is the gathering in of living stones into the one
true Church. How little are we told in God's Word about
unconverted men compared with what we are told about
believers! The history of Nimrod, the mighty hunter, is
dismissed in a few words. The history of Abraham, the

father of the faithful, occupies several chapters. Nothing in Scripture is so important as the concerns of the true Church. The world takes up little of God's Word. The Church and its story take up much.

For ever let us thank God, my beloved brethren, that the building of the one true Church is laid on the shoulders of One that is mighty. Let us bless God that it does not rest upon man. Let us bless God that it does not depend on missionaries, ministers, or committees. Christ is the almighty Builder. He will carry on His work, though nations and visible Churches do not know their duty. Christ will never fail. That which He hath undertaken He will certainly accomplish.

III. – I pass on to the third point, which I proposed to consider – The *Foundation* upon which this Church is built. The Lord Jesus Christ tells us, 'Upon this Rock will I build My Church.'

What did the Lord Jesus Christ mean, when He spoke of this foundation? Did He mean the Apostle Peter, to whom He was speaking? I think assuredly not. I can see no reason, if he meant Peter, why He did not say, 'Upon thee' will I build My Church. If He had meant Peter, He would have said, I will build My Church on thee, as plainly as He said, 'to thee will I give the keys.' No! it was not the person of the Apostle Peter, but the good confession which the Apostle had just made. It was not Peter, the erring, unstable man; but the mighty truth which the Father had revealed to Peter. It was the truth concerning Jesus Christ himself which was the Rock. It was Christ's Mediatorship, and Christ's Messiahship. It was the blessed truth, that Jesus was the promised Saviour, the true Surety, the real Intercessor between God and man. This was the rock, and this

[16]

the foundation upon which the Church of Christ was to be built.

My brethren, this foundation was laid at a mighty cost. It needed that the Son of God should take our nature upon Him, and in that nature live, suffer, and die, not for His own sins, but for ours. It needed that in that nature Christ should go to the grave, and rise again. It needed that in that nature Christ should go up to heaven, to sit at the right hand of God, having obtained eternal redemption for all His people. No other foundation but this could have borne the weight of that Church of which our text speaks. No other foundation could have met the necessities of a world of sinners.

That foundation once obtained, is very strong. It can bear the weight of the sin of all the world. It has borne the weight of all the sins of all the believers who have built on it. Sins of thought, sins of the imagination, sins of the heart, sins of the head, sins which every one has seen, and sins which no man knows, sins against God, and sins against man, sins of all kinds and descriptions, – that mighty rock can bear the weight of all these sins and not give way. The mediatorial office of Christ is a remedy sufficient for all the sins of all the world.

To this one foundation every member of Christ's true Church is joined. In many things believers are disunited and disagreed. In the matter of their soul's foundation they are all of one mind. They are all built on the rock. Ask where they get their peace, and hope, and joyful expectation of good things to come. You would find that all flows from that one mighty truth, – Christ the Mediator between God and man, and the office that Christ holds, as the High-priest and Surety of sinners.

Here is the point which demands our personal attention. Are we upon the rock? Are we really joined to the one foundation? What says that good old divine, Archbishop Leighton? 'God has laid this precious stone for this very purpose, that weary sinners may rest upon it. The multitude of imaginary believers lie round about it, but they are none the better for that, any more than stones that lie loose in heaps, near a foundation, but not joined unto it. There is no benefit to us by Christ, without union with Him.'

Look to your foundation, my beloved brethren, if you would know whether or not you are members of the one true Church. It is a point that may be known to yourselves. Your public worship we can see, but we cannot see whether you are personally built upon the rock. Your attendance at the Lord's table we can see, but we cannot see whether you are joined to Christ, and one with Christ, and Christ in you. But all shall come to light one day. The secrets of all hearts shall be exposed. Perhaps you go to church regularly, you love your Prayer-book, you are constant in attending on every means of grace your Church supplies. All this is right and good, so far as it goes. But all this time, see that you make no mistake about your own personal salvation. See that your own soul is upon the rock. Without this, all else is nothing. Without this, you will never stand in the day of judgment. Better a thousand times in that day to be found in a cottage upon the rock, than in a palace upon the sand!

IV. – I proceed, in the fourth place, to speak of the *Implied Trials* of the Church, to which our text refers. There is mention made of 'the gates of hell.' By that expression we are meant to understand the power of the devil!

The history of Christ's true Church has always been one of conflict and war. It has been constantly assailed by a deadly enemy, Satan, the prince of this world. The devil hates the true Church of Christ with an undying hatred. He is ever stirring up opposition against all its members. He is ever urging the children of this world to do his will, and injure and harass the people of God. If he cannot bruise the head, he will bruise the heel. If he cannot rob believers of heaven, he will vex them by the way.

For six thousand years this enmity has gone on. Millions of the ungodly have been the devil's agents, and done the devil's work, though they knew it not. The Pharaohs, the Herods, the Neros, the Julians, the Diocletians, the bloody Marys – what were they all but Satan's tools, when they persecuted the disciples of Jesus Christ.

Warfare with the powers of hell has been the experience of the whole body of Christ. It has always been a bush burning, though not consumed – a woman fleeing into the wilderness, but not swallowed up. The visible Churches have their times of prosperity and seasons of peace, but never has there been a time of peace for the true Church. Its conflict is perpetual. Its battle never ends.

Warfare with the powers of hell is the experience of every individual member of the true Church. Each has to fight. What are the lives of all the saints, but records of battles? What were such men as Paul, and James, and Peter, and John, and Polycarp, and Ignatius, and Augustine, and Luther, and Calvin, and Latimer, and Baxter, but soldiers engaged in a constant warfare? Sometimes their persons have been assailed, and sometimes their property. Sometimes they have been harassed by calumnies and slanders, and sometimes by open persecution. But in one way or another the devil has been continually warring against the Church. The 'gates of hell' have been continually assaulting the people of Christ.

Men and brethren, we who preach the Gospel can hold out to all who come to Christ, exceeding great and precious promises. We can offer boldly to you in our Master's name, the peace of God which passeth all understanding. Mercy, free grace, and full salvation, are offered to every one who will come to Christ, and believe on Him. But we promise you no peace with the world, or with the devil. We warn you, on the contrary, that there must be warfare, so long as you are in the body. We would not keep you back, or deter you from Christ's service. But we would have you 'count the cost,' and fully understand what Christ's service entails. Hell is behind you. Heaven is before you. Home lies on the other side of a troubled sea. Thousands, tens of thousands have crossed these stormy waters, and in spite of all opposition, have reached the haven where they would be. Hell has assailed them, but has not prevailed. Go forward, beloved brethren, and fear not the adversary. Only abide in Christ, and the victory is sure.

Marvel not at the enmity of the gates of hell. 'If ye were of the world, the world would love his own.' So long as the world is the world, and the devil the devil, so long there must be warfare, and believers in Christ must be soldiers. The world hated Christ, and the world will hate true Christians, as long as the earth stands. As the great reformer, Luther, said, 'Cain will go on murdering Abel so long as the Church is on earth.'

Be prepared for the enmity of the gates of hell. Put on the whole armour of God. The tower of David contains a thousand bucklers, all ready for the use of God's people. The weapons of our warfare have been tried by millions of poor sinners like ourselves, and have never been found to fail.

Be patient under the enmity of the gates of hell. It is all working together for your good. It tends to sanctify. It keeps you awake. It makes you humble. It drives you nearer to the Lord Jesus Christ. It weans you from the world. It helps to make you pray more. Above all, it makes you long for heaven, and say with heart as well as lips, 'Come, Lord Jesus.'

Be not cast down by the enmity of hell. The warfare of the true child of God is as much a mark of grace as the inward peace which he enjoys. No cross, no crown! No conflict, no saving Christianity! 'Blessed are ye,' said our Lord Jesus Christ, 'when men shall revile you, and persecute you, and say all manner of evil against you falsely, for My sake.'

V. – There remains one thing more to be considered: the *Security* of the true Church of Christ. There is a glorious promise given by the mighty Builder, 'The gates of hell shall not prevail against it.' He who cannot lie has pledged His royal word, that all the powers of hell shall never overthrow His Church. It shall continue, and stand, in spite of every assault. It shall never be overcome. All other created things perish and pass away, but not the Church of Christ. The hand of outward violence, or the moth of inward decay, prevail over everything else, but not over the temple that Christ builds.

Empires have risen and fallen in rapid succession. Egypt, Assyria, Babylon, Persia, Tyre, Carthage, Rome, Greece, Venice – where are all these now? They were all the creations of man's hand, and have passed away. But the Church of Christ lives on.

The mightiest cities have become heaps of ruins. The

broad walls of Babylon are sunk to the ground. The palaces of Nineveh are mounds of dust. The hundred gates of Thebes are only matters of history. Tyre is a place where fishermen hang their nets. Carthage is a desolation. Yet all this time the true Church stands. The gates of hell do not prevail against it.

The earliest visible Churches have in many cases decayed and perished. Where is the Church of Ephesus and the Church of Antioch? Where is the Church of Alexandria and the Church of Constantinople? Where are the Corinthian, and Philippian, and Thessalonian Churches? Where, indeed, are they all? They departed from the Word of God. They were proud of their bishops, and synods, and ceremonies, and learning, and antiquity. They did not glory in the true cross of Christ. They did not hold fast the Gospel. They did not give Jesus His rightful office, or faith its rightful place. They are now among the things that have been. Their candlestick has been taken away. But all this time the true Church has lived on.

Has the true Church been oppressed in one country? It has fled to another. Has it been trampled on and oppressed in one soil? It has taken root and flourished in some other climate. Fire, sword, prisons, fines, penalties, have never been able to destroy its vitality. Its persecutors have died and gone to their own place, but the Word of God has lived, and grown and multiplied. Weak as this true Church may appear to the eye of man, it is an anvil which has broken many a hammer in times past, and perhaps will break many more before the end. He that lays hands on it, is touching the apple of God's eye.

The promise of our text is true of the whole body of the true Church. Christ will never be without a witness in the world. He has had a people in the worst of times. He had seven thousand in Israel even in the days of Ahab. There are some now, I believe, in the dark places of the Roman and Greek Churches, who, in spite of much weakness, are serving Christ. The devil may rage horribly. The Church may in some countries be brought exceedingly low. But the gates of hell shall never entirely prevail.

The promise of our text is true of every individual member of the Church. Some of God's people have been brought very low, so that they despaired of their safety. Some have fallen sadly, as David and Peter did. Some have departed from the faith for a time, like Cranmer and Jewell. Many have been tried by cruel doubts and fears. But all have got safe home at last, the youngest as well as the oldest, the weakest as well as the strongest. And so it will be to the end. Can you prevent to-morrow's sun from rising? Can you prevent the tide in the Bristol Channel from ebbing and flowing? Can you prevent the planets moving in their respective orbits? Then, and then alone, can you prevent the salvation of any believer, however feeble, – of any living stone in that Church which is built upon the rock, however small or insignificant that stone may appear.

The true Church is Christ's body. Not one bone in that mystical body shall ever be broken. – The true Church is Christ's bride. They whom God hath joined in everlasting covenant, shall never be put asunder. – The true Church is Christ's flock. When the lion came and took a lamb out of David's flock, David arose and delivered the lamb from his mouth. Christ will do the same. He is David's greater son. Not a single sick lamb in Christ's flock shall perish. He will say to His Father in the last day, 'Of those whom Thou gavest Me I have lost none.' – The true Church is the wheat of the earth. It may be sifted, winnowed, buffeted, tossed to and fro. But not one grain shall be lost. The tares and chaff shall be burned. The wheat shall be gathered into the barn. – The true Church is Christ's army. The Captain of our salvation loses none of his soldiers. His plans are never defeated. His supplies never fail. His muster roll is the same at the end as it was at the beginning. Of the men that marched gallantly out of England a few years ago in the Crimean war, how many never came back! Regiments that went forth, strong and cheerful, with bands playing and banners flying, laid their bones in a foreign land, and never returned to their native country. But it is not so with Christ's army. Not one of His soldiers shall be missing at last. He Himself declares 'They shall never perish.'

The devil may cast some of the members of the true Church into prison. He may kill, and burn, and torture, and hang. But after he has killed the body, there is nothing more that he can do. He cannot hurt the soul. When the French troops took Rome a few years ago, they found on the walls of a prison cell, under the Inquisition, the words of a prisoner. Who he was, we know not. But his words are worthy of remembrance. Though dead, he yet speaketh. He had written on the walls, very likely after an unjust trial, and a still more unjust excommunication, the following striking words: – 'Blessed Jesus, they cannot cast me out of Thy true Church.' That record is true. Not all the power of Satan can cast out of Christ's true Church one single believer.

The children of this world may wage fierce warfare against the Church, but they cannot stop the work of conversion. What said the sneering Emperor Julian, in the early ages of the Church – 'What is the carpenter's son doing now?' An aged Christian made answer, 'He is making a coffin for Julian himself.' But a few months passed away, when Julian, with all his pomp and power, died in battle. Where was Christ when the fires of Smithfield were lighted, and when Latimer and Ridley were burnt at the stake? What was Christ doing then? He was still carrying on His work of building. That work will ever go on, even in troublous times.

Fear not, beloved brethren, to begin serving Christ. He to whom you commit your souls has all power in heaven and earth, and He will keep you. He will never let you be cast away. Relatives may oppose. Neighbours may mock. The world may slander and sneer. Fear not! Fear not! The powers of hell shall never prevail against your soul. Greater is He that is for you, than all they that are against you.

Fear not for the Church of Christ, my brethren, when ministers die, and saints are taken away. Christ can ever maintain His own cause, He will raise up better and brighter stars. The stars are all in His right hand. Leave off all anxious thought about the future. Cease to be cast down by the measures of statesmen, or the plots of wolves in sheep's clothing. Christ will ever provide for His own Church. Christ will take care that the gates of hell shall not prevail against it. All is going on well, though our eyes may not see it. The kingdoms of this world shall yet become the kingdoms of our God and of His Christ.

Suffer me now to say a few words of practical application of this sermon. I speak to many, whom I speak to for the first time. I speak, perhaps, to many whom I speak to for the last time. Let not this service conclude without an effort to press home the sermon on each heart.

1. My first word of application shall be a question. What shall that question be? Wherewith shall I approach you? What shall I ask? I ask you, whether you are a member of

the one true Church of Christ? Are you in the highest, the best sense, a 'Churchman' in the sight of God? You know what I mean. I look far beyond the Church of England. I speak of the Church built upon the rock. I ask you, with all solemnity – Are you a member of that one Church of Christ? Are you joined to the great Foundation? Have you received the Holy Ghost? Does the Spirit witness with your spirit, that you are one with Christ, and Christ with you? I beseech you, in the name of God, to lay to heart this question, and to ponder it well.

Take heed to yourselves, dear brethren, if you cannot give a satisfactory answer to my inquiry. Take heed, take heed, that you do not make shipwreck of faith. Take heed, lest at last the gates of hell prevail against you, the devil claim you as his own, and you be cast away for ever. Take heed, lest you go down to the pit from the land of Bibles, and in the full light of Christ's Gospel.

2. My second word of application shall be an invitation. I address it to all who are not yet true believers. I say to you, Come and join the one true Church without delay. Come and join yourselves to the Lord Jesus Christ in an everlasting covenant not to be forgotten. Come to Christ and be saved. The day of decision must come some time. Why not this very evening? Why not to-day, while it is called to-day? – Why not this very night, ere the sun rises to-morrow morning? – Come to Him, whose I am, and whom I serve. Come to my Master, Jesus Christ. Come, I say, for all things are now ready. Mercy is ready for you, heaven is ready for you, angels are ready to rejoice over you, Christ is ready to receive you. Christ will receive you gladly, and welcome you among His children. Come into the ark – the flood of God's wrath will soon break upon the earth – come into the ark and be safe.

Come into the life-boat. The old world will soon break into pieces! Hear you not the tremblings of it? The world is but a wreck hard upon the sandbank. The night is far-spent – the waves are beginning to rise – the winds are rising – the storm will soon shatter the old wreck. But the life-boat is launched, and we, the ministers of the Gospel, beseech you to come into the life-boat and be saved.

Dost thou ask, How can I come, my sins are so many? Dost thou ask how thou shalt come? Hear the words of that beautiful hymn: –

> 'Just as I am: without one plea,
> But that Thy blood was shed for me,
> And that Thou bid'st me come to Thee, –
> O Lamb of God I come.'

That is the way to come to Christ. You should come, waiting for nothing, and tarrying for nothing. You should come, as a hungry sinner, to be filled, – as a poor sinner to be enriched, – as a bad, undeserving sinner to be clothed with righteousness. So coming, Christ would receive you. 'Him that cometh' to Christ, He 'will in no wise cast out.' Oh! come, come to Jesus Christ.

3. Last of all, let me given a word of exhortation to my believing hearers.

Live a holy life, my brethren. Walk worthy of the Church to which you belong. Live like citizens of heaven. Let your light shine before men, so that the world may profit by your conduct. Let them know whose you are, and whom you serve. Be epistles of Christ, known and read of all men; written in such clear letters, that none can say, I know not whether he be a member of Christ or not.

Live a courageous life, my brethren. Confess Christ before men. Whatever station you occupy, in that station confess Christ. Why should you be ashamed of Him? He was not ashamed of you on the cross. He is ready to confess you now before His Father in heaven. Why should you be ashamed of Him? Be bold. Be very bold. The good soldier is not ashamed of his uniform. The true believer ought never to be ashamed of Christ.

Live a joyful life, my brethren. Live like men who look for that blessed hope – the second coming of Jesus Christ. This is the prospect to which we should all look forward. It is not so much the thought of going to heaven, as of heaven coming to us, that should fill our minds. There is a good time coming for all the people of God – a good time for all the Church of Christ – a good time for all believers – a bad time for the impenitent and unbelieving – a bad time for them that will serve their own lusts, and turn their backs on the Lord, but a good time for true Christians. For that good time, let us wait, and watch, and pray.

The scaffolding will soon be taken down – the last stone will soon be brought out – the top-stone will be placed upon the edifice. Yet a little time, and the full beauty of the building shall be clearly seen.

The great master Builder will soon come himself. A building shall be shown to assembled worlds, in which there shall be no imperfection. The Saviour and the saved shall rejoice together. The whole universe shall acknowledge, that in the building of Christ's Church all was well done.

2: 'Not Corrupting the Word'*

*'For we are not as many, which corrupt the word of
God: but as of sincerity, but as of God, in the
sight of God speak we in Christ'* (2 Cor. 2:17).

IT IS NO LIGHT MATTER TO SPEAK TO ANY AS-
sembly of immortal souls about the things of God. But
the most serious of all responsibilities is, to speak to a
gathering of ministers, such as that which I now see before
me. The awful feeling will come across my mind, that one
single word said wrong, sinking into some heart, and
bearing fruit at some future time, in some pulpit, may
lead to harm, of which we cannot know the extent.

But there are occasions when true humility is to be seen,
not so much in loud professions of our weakness, as in
forgetting ourselves altogether. I desire to forget self at
this time, in turning my attention to this portion of Scripture. If I say little about my own sense of insufficiency, do
me the justice to believe, that it is not because I do not
feel it much.

The Greek expression, which we have translated, 'corrupt,' is derived from a word, the etymology of which is not
quite agreed on by lexicographers. It either means a trades-
man, who does his business dishonestly, or a vintner, who
adulterates the wine which he exposes for sale. Wycliffe
renders it by an obsolete phrase – 'We are not of those who
do avoutry the Word of God.' Tyndale renders it – 'We are

---

* This address was delivered at an aggregate Clerical Meeting, held at
Weston-super-Mare, in August, 1858, under the presidency of Archdeacon Law. The reader will kindly remember that neither of these
addresses were written, and that he has before him a reporter's notes
corrected.

not of those who chop and change the Word of God.' The Rhemish version is – 'We are not as many, who adulterate the Word of God.' In our margin we read – 'We are not as many, who deal deceitfully with the Word of God.'

In the construction of the sentence, the Holy Ghost has inspired St. Paul to use both the negative and the positive way of stating the truth. This mode of construction adds clearness and unmistakableness to the meaning of the words, and intensity and strength to the assertion, which they contain. Instances of a similar construction occur in three other remarkable passages of Scripture, two on the subject of baptism, one on the subject of the new birth. (John 1:13; 1 Peter 1:23; 1 Peter 3:21.) It will be found, therefore, that there are contained in the text both negative and positive lessons for the instruction of the ministers of Christ. Some things we ought to avoid. Others we ought to follow.

The first of the negative lessons is, a plain warning against corrupting or dealing deceitfully with the Word of God. The Apostle says, 'many' do it, pointing out to us that even in his time there were those who did not deal faithfully and honestly with God's truth. Here is a full answer to those who assert that the primitive Church was one of unmixed purity. The mystery of iniquity had already begun to work. The lesson which we are taught is, to beware of all dishonest statements of that Word of God which we are commissioned to preach. We are to add nothing to it. We are to take nothing away.

Now when can it be said of us, that we corrupt the Word of God in the present day? What are the rocks and shoals which we ought to shun, if we would not be of the 'many' who deal deceitfully with God's truth? A few suggestions on this head may not be without use.

We corrupt the Word of God most dangerously, when we throw any doubt on the plenary inspiration of any part of Holy Scripture. This is not merely corrupting the cup, but the whole fountain. This is not merely corrupting the bucket of living water, which we profess to present to our people, but poisoning the whole well. Once wrong on this point, the whole substance of our religion is in danger. It is a flaw in the foundation. It is a worm at the root of our theology. Once allow this worm to gnaw the root, and we must not be surprised if the branches, the leaves, and the fruit, little by little decay. The whole subject of inspiration, I am well aware, is surrounded with difficulty. All I would say is, that, in my humble judgment, notwithstanding some difficulties which we may not be able now to solve, the only safe and tenable ground to maintain is this, – that every chapter, and every verse, and every word in the Bible has been 'given by inspiration of God.' We should never desert a great principle in theology any more than in science, because of apparent difficulties which we are not able at present to remove.

Suffer me to mention an illustration of this important axiom. Those conversant with astronomy know, that before the discovery of the planet Neptune there were difficulties, which greatly troubled the most scientific astronomers, respecting certain aberrations of the planet Uranus. These aberrations puzzled the minds of astronomers, and some of them suggested that they might possibly prove the whole Newtonian system to be untrue. But at that time a well-known French astronomer, named Leverrier, read before the Academy of Science a paper, in which he laid down this great axiom, – that it did not become a scientific man to give up a principle because of difficulties which could not be explained. He said in effect, 'We cannot explain the aberrations of Uranus now; but we may be sure that the Newtonian system will be proved to be right, sooner or later. Something may be discovered one day, which will prove that these aberrations may be accounted for, and yet the Newtonian system remain true and unshaken.' A few years after, the anxious eyes of astronomers discovered the last great planet, Neptune. The planet was shown to be the true cause of all the aberrations of Uranus; and what the French astronomer had laid down as a principle in science, was proved to be wise and true. The application of the anecdote is obvious. Let us beware of giving up any first principle in theology. Let us not give up the great principle of plenary inspiration because of difficulties. The day may come when they will all be solved. In the mean time we may rest assured that the difficulties which beset any other theory of inspiration are tenfold greater than any which beset our own.

Secondly, we corrupt the Word of God when we make defective statements of doctrine. We do so when we add to the Bible the opinions of the Church, or of the Fathers, as if they were of equal authority. We do so when we take away from the Bible, for the sake of pleasing men; or, from a feeling of false liberality, keep back any statement which seems narrow, and harsh, or hard. We do so when we try to soften down anything that is taught about eternal punishment, or the reality of hell. We do so when we bring forward doctrines in their wrong proportions. We have all our favourite doctrines, and our minds are so constituted that it is hard to see one truth very clearly without forgetting that there are other truths equally important. We must not forget the exhortation of Paul, – to minister 'according to the proportion of faith.' We do so when we exhibit an excessive anxiety to fence, and guard, and qualify such doctrines as justification by faith without the deeds of the law, for fear of the charge of antinomianism; or when we flinch from strong statements about holiness, for fear of being thought legal. We do so, not least, when we shrink from the use of Bible language in giving an account of doctrines. We are apt to keep back such expressions as 'born again,' 'election,' 'adoption,' 'conversion,' 'assurance,' and to use a roundabout phraseology, as if we were ashamed of plain Bible words. I cannot expand these statements, for want of time. I content myself with mentioning them, and leave them to your private thought.

In the third place, we corrupt the Word of God when we make a defective practical application of it. We do so when we do not discriminate between classes in our congregations – when we address all as being possessed of grace, by reason of their baptism or church-membership, and do not draw the line between those who have the Spirit and those who have not. Are we not apt to keep back plain home appeals to the unconverted? When we have eighteen hundred or two thousand persons before our pulpits, a vast proportion of whom we must know are unconverted, are we not apt to say, 'Now if there be any one of you who does not know the things that are for his eternal peace' – when we ought rather to say, 'If there be any of you who has not the grace of God in him'? – And are we not in danger of defective handling of the Word in our practical exhortations, by not bringing home the statements of the Bible to the various classes in our congregations? We speak plainly to the poor; but do we also speak plainly to the rich? Do we speak plainly in our dealings with the upper classes? This is a point on which, I fear, we need to search our consciences.

I now turn to the positive lessons which the text contains. 'As of sincerity, as of God, in the sight of God, speak we in Christ.' A few words on each head must suffice.

We should aim to speak 'as of sincerity' – sincerity of aim, heart, and motive; to speak as those who are thoroughly convinced of the truth of what they say; as those who have a deep feeling and tender love for those whom we address.

We should aim to speak 'as of God.' We ought to strive to feel like men commissioned to speak for God, and on His behalf. In our dread of running into Romanism, we too often forget the language of the Apostle – 'I magnify mine office.' We forget how great is the responsibility of the New Testament minister, and how awful the sin of those who when a real messenger of Christ addresses them refuse to receive his message, and harden their hearts against it.

We should aim to speak as 'in the sight of God.' We are to ask ourselves, not, What did the people think of me? but, What was I in the sight of God? Latimer was once called upon to preach before Henry VIII., and began his sermon in the following manner. (I quote from memory, and do not pretend to verbal accuracy.) He began: 'Latimer! Latimer! dost thou remember thou art speaking before the high and mighty King Henry VIII.; before him who has power to command thee to be sent to prison; before him who can have thy head struck off, if it please him? Wilt thou not take care to say nothing that will offend royal ears?' Then after a pause, he went on: 'Latimer! Latimer! dost not thou remember that thou art speaking before the King of kings and Lord of lords; before Him, at whose bar Henry VIII. will stand; before Him, to whom one day thou wilt have to give account thyself? Latimer! Latimer! be faithful to thy Master, and declare all God's Word.' O, that this may be the spirit in which we may ever retire from our pulpits, – not caring whether men are pleased or displeased, not caring whether men say we were eloquent or feeble; but going away with the witness of our conscience – I have spoken as in God's sight.

Finally, we should aim to speak 'as in Christ.' The meaning of this phrase is doubtful. Grotius says, 'We are to speak as in His name, as ambassadors.' But Grotius is poor authority. – Beza says, 'We are to speak about Christ, concerning Christ.' This is good doctrine, but hardly the meaning of the words. – Others say, We are to speak as ourselves joined to Christ, as those who have received mercy from Christ, and whose only title to address others is from Christ alone. – Others say, We should speak as through Christ, in the strength of Christ. No meaning, perhaps, is better than this. The expression in the Greek exactly answers to Phil. 4: 13. 'I can do all things through Christ, which strengtheneth me.' Whatever sense we ascribe to these words, one thing is clear: we should speak in Christ, as those who have themselves received mercy; as those who desire to exalt, not themselves, but the Saviour; and as those who care nothing what men think of them, so long as Christ is magnified in their ministry.

In conclusion, we should all inquire, Do we ever handle the Word of God deceitfully? Do we realize what it is to speak as of God, as in the sight of God, and in Christ? Let me put to all one searching question. Is there any text in God's Word which we shrink from expounding? Is there any statement in the Bible which we avoid speaking about to our people, not because we do not understand it, but because it contradicts some pet notion of ours as to what is truth? If it be so, let us ask our consciences whether this be not very like handling the Word of God deceitfully.

Is there anything in the Bible we keep back for fear of seeming harsh, and of giving offence to some of our hearers? Is there any statement, either doctrinal or practical, which we mangle, mutilate or dismember? If so, are we dealing honestly with God's Word?

Let us pray to be kept from corrupting God's Word. Let neither fear nor favour of man induce us to keep back, or avoid, or change, or mutilate, or qualify any text in the Bible. Surely we ought to have holy boldness when we speak as ambassadors of God. We have no reason to be ashamed of any statement we make in our pulpits so long as it is Scriptural. I have often thought that one great secret of the marvellous honour which God has put on a man who is not in our communion (I allude to Mr Spurgeon) – is, the extraordinary boldness and confidence with which he stands up in the pulpit to speak to people about their sins and their souls. It cannot be said he does it from fear of any, or to please any. He seems to give every class of hearers its portion, – to the rich and the poor, the high and the low, the peer and the peasant, the learned and the illiterate. He gives to every one plain dealing, according to God's Word. I believe that very boldness has much to do with the success which God is pleased to give to his ministry. Let us not be ashamed to learn a lesson from him in this respect. Let us go and do likewise.

3: 'Give Thyself Wholly to Them'*

'Give thyself wholly to them' (1 Tim. 4:15).

I NEED HARDLY REMIND YOU, THAT THE GREEK expression which we have translated, 'give thyself wholly to them,' is somewhat remarkable. It would be more literally rendered, 'Be in these things.' It answers to the Latin phrases, 'totus in illis,' and 'omnis in hôc sum.' We have nothing exactly corresponding to the expression in our language, and the words which our translators have chosen are perhaps as well calculated as any to convey the idea which was put by the Holy Ghost in St Paul's mind.

When the Apostle says, 'give thyself wholly to these things,' he seems to look at the 'things' of which he had been speaking in the preceding verses, beginning with the words 'Be thou an example of the believers, in word, in conversation, in charity, in spirit, in faith, in purity.'

We have here a mark set before the ministers of the New Testament, at which we are all to aim, and of which we must all feel we come short. Yet it is an old saying, 'He that aims high is the most likely to strike high; and he that shoots at the moon will shoot further than the man who shoots at the bush.'

The Apostle appears to me to suggest that the minister must be a man of one thing: to use his own words, a 'man of God.' We hear of men of business, and men of pleasure, and men of science. The aim of the minister should be, to be 'a man of God;' or to employ a phrase

* An address delivered at the aggregate clerical meeting, at Weston-super-Mare, in August, 1859.

used in some heathen countries, to be 'Jesus Christ's man.' An expression is sometimes used with reference to the army, which we may apply to the soldiers of the Great Captain of our salvation. Some men are said to be 'drawing-room soldiers,' and 'carpet knights.' They are said to have entered the army for the sake of the uniform, and for no other cause. But there are many of whom public opinion says, such a man is 'every inch a soldier.' This should be the aim which we should place before us; we should seek to be 'every inch the minister of Jesus Christ.' We should aim to be the same men at all times, in all positions, and places; not on Sunday only, but on week days also; not merely in the pulpit, but everywhere – in the drawing-room of the rich, by our own fire-side, and in the cottage of the poor man. There are those, of whom their congregations have said, that when they were in the pulpit they never wished them to come out, and when they went out they never wished them to go in. May God give us all grace to lay that to heart! May we seek so to live, so to preach, so to work, so to give ourselves wholly to the business of our calling, that this bitter remark may never be made upon us. Our profession is a very peculiar one. Others have their seasons of relaxation, when they can altogether lay aside their work. This can never be done by the faithful minister of Jesus Christ. Once put on, his office must never be put off. At home, abroad, taking relaxation, going to the sea side, he must ever carry his business with him. A great lawyer could say of his official robes, 'Lie there, Lord Chancellor.' Such ought never to be the mind of the minister of Christ.

There are some things which the high demand of this text suggests, as needful to be followed after and practised.

It demands, firstly, entire devotion to the great work to

which we are ordained. When one was commanded by the Saviour to follow Him, he replied, 'Suffer me first to bury my father;' but then there came that solemn saying, 'Let the dead bury their dead; but go thou and preach the Gospel.' – 'Suffer me first to bid them farewell who are at my house,' said another; and to him there came the remarkable sentence, 'no man having put his hand to the plough, and looking back, is fit for the kingdom of God.' – 'Salute no man by the way,' was Christ's charge to the seventy disciples. Surely these Scriptural expressions teach us, that in all our dealings in our office, we must have a high standard. We must strive to be men of one thing – that thing being the work of Jesus Christ.

It demands, secondly, a thorough separation from the things of the world. I hold it to be of the greatest importance to keep the ministerial office, so far as we can, distinct and separate from everything that is secular. I trust we shall hear every year of fewer and fewer ministers of the Gospel who are magistrates, and fewer and fewer ministers who take part in agricultural meetings, and win prizes for fat pigs, enormous bullocks, and large crops of turnips. There is no apostolical succession in such avocations. Nor yet is this all. We should be separated from the pleasures of the world, as well as from its business. There are many innocent and indifferent amusements, for which the minister of Christ ought to have no time. He ought to say, 'I have no leisure for these things. I am doing a great work, and I cannot come down.'

It demands, thirdly, a jealous watchfulness over our own social conduct. We ought not to be always paying morning calls of courtesy and dining out, as others do. It will not do to say, that our Lord went to a marriage feast, and sat at meat in the pharisee's house, and therefore we may do the same. I only reply, Let us go in His spirit, with His faithfulness and boldness, to say a word in season, and to give the conversation a profitable turn, and then we may go with safety. Unless we do this, we should be careful where we go, with whom we sit down, and where we spend our evenings. There was a quaint saying of John Wesley to his ministers, which Cecil quotes, as containing the germ of much truth. 'Don't aim at being thought gentlemen; you have no more to do with being gentlemen than with being dancing-masters.' Our aim should be not to be regarded as agreeable persons at the dinner table, but to be known everywhere as faithful, consistent ministers of Jesus Christ.

It demands, fourthly, a diligent redemption of time. We should give attention to reading, every day that we live. We should strive to bring all our reading to bear on our work. We ought to keep our eyes open continually, and be ever picking up matter for our sermons, – as we travel by the way, as we sit by the fire-side, as we are standing on the platform at the railway station. We should be keeping in our mind's eye our Master's business, – observing, noting, looking out, gathering up something that will throw fresh light on our work, and enable us to put the truth in a more striking way. He that looks out for something to learn will always be able to learn something.

Having suggested these things, I will next proceed to ask, What will be the consequence of our giving ourselves wholly to these things? Remember, we shall not receive the praise of men. We shall be thought extreme, and ascetic, and righteous over much. Those who want to serve God and serve mammon at the same time, will think our standard too high, our practice too stringent. They will say, that we are going too far and too fast for a world such as that in which we live. May we never care what men say of us, so long as we walk in the light of God's Word! May we strive and pray to be wholly independent of, and indifferent to man's opinion, so long as we please God! May we remember the woe pronounced by our Master, when He said, 'Woe be unto you, when all men shall speak well of you,' and the words of St Paul, 'If I yet pleased men, I should not be the servant of Christ.'

But though 'giving ourselves wholly to these things' we shall not win the praise of men, we shall attain the far more important end of usefulness to souls. I acknowledge to the full, the doctrine of the sovereignty of God in the salvation of sinners. I acknowledge that those who preach best, and live nearest to God, have not always been honoured in their lives to the saving of many souls. But still, the man who is most entirely and wholly Jesus Christ's man – a man of one thing, who lives Sunday and weekday, everywhere, at home and abroad, as a man whose single endeavour is to give himself to the work of Jesus Christ – this is the man, this is the minister, who will generally, in the long run, do most good. The case of Mr. Simeon will apply here. You all know how he was persecuted when he began to testify for Christ, in Cambridge. You know how many there were who would not speak to him, how the finger of scorn was pointed at him continually. But we know how he went on persevering in the work, and how, when he died, all Cambridge came forth to give him honour, and how heads of houses, and fellows of colleges, and men who had scoffed at him while he lived, honoured him at his death. They testified, that the life he had lived had had its effect, and that they had seen and known that God was with him. I once saw in Dundee one who had known much of that godly man, Robert M'Cheyne. She told me that those who read his letters and sermons had a very faint idea of what he was. She said to me, 'If you have read all his works, you just know nothing at all about him. You must have seen the man, and heard him, and known him, and have been in company with him, to know what a man of God he was.'

Furthermore, giving ourselves wholly to these things will bring happiness and peace to our consciences. I speak now amongst friends, and not amongst worldly people, where I should need to fence and guard and explain what I mean. I shall not be suspected of holding justification by works by those I see before me. I speak of such a good conscience as the Apostle refers to: We trust we have a 'good conscience.' (Heb. 13:18). To have this good conscience is clearly bound up with high aims, high motives, a high standard of ministerial life and practice. I am quite sure, that the more we give ourselves wholly to the work of the ministry, the more inward happiness, the greater sense of the light of God's countenance, are we likely to enjoy.

The subject is a deeply humbling one. Who does not feel, 'My leanness, my leanness! my unprofitableness! How far short I come of this high standard!'? What reason have we, having received mercy, not to faint! What reason have we, having been spared by God's long suffering, to abound in the work of the Lord, and to give ourselves wholly to our business! The grand secret is, to be ever looking to Jesus, and living a life of close communion with Him. At Cambridge, the other day, I saw a picture of Henry Martyn, bequeathed by Mr. Simeon to the public library. A friend informed me that that picture used to hang in Mr. Simeon's room, and that when he was disposed to trifle in the work of the ministry, he used to stand before it and say, 'It seems to say to me, Charles Simeon, don't trifle, don't trifle; Charles Simeon, remember whose you are, and whom you serve.' And then the worthy man, in his own peculiar way, would bow respectfully, and say, 'I will not trifle, I will not trifle; I will not forget.'

May we, in conclusion, look to a far higher pattern than any man, – Martyn, M'Cheyne, or any other. May we look to the Great Chief Shepherd, the great pattern, in whose steps we are to walk! May we abide in Him, and never trifle! May we hold on our way, looking to Jesus, keeping clear of the world, its pleasures, and its follies, – caring nothing for the world's frowns, and not much moved by the world's smiles, – looking forward to that day when the Great Shepherd shall give to all who have done His work, and preached His Gospel, a crown of glory that fadeth not away! The more we have the mind of Christ, the more we shall understand what it is to 'give ourselves wholly to these things.'

4: Pharisees and Sadducees

'Then Jesus said unto them, Take heed and beware of the leaven of the Pharisees and of the Sadducees' (Matt. 16:6).

EVERY WORD SPOKEN BY THE LORD JESUS IS FULL of deep instruction for Christians. It is the voice of the Chief Shepherd. It is the Great Head of the Church speaking to all its members, – the King of kings speaking to His subjects, – the Master of the house speaking to His servants, – the Captain of our salvation speaking to His soldiers. Above all, it is the voice of Him who said, 'I have not spoken of Myself: the Father which sent Me, He gave Me a commandment what I should say and what I should speak.' (John 12:49.) The heart of every believer in the Lord Jesus ought to burn within him when he hears his Master's words: he ought to say, 'This is the voice of my beloved.' (Cant. 2:8.)

And every kind of word spoken by the Lord Jesus is of the greatest value. Precious as gold are all His words of doctrine and precept; precious are all His parables and prophecies; precious are all His words of comfort and of consolation; precious, not least, are all His words of caution and of warning. We are not merely to hear Him when He says, 'Come unto me, all ye that labour, and are heavy laden;' we are to hear Him also when He says, 'Take heed and beware.'

I am going to direct attention to one of the most solemn and emphatic warnings which the Lord Jesus ever delivered: 'Take heed and beware of the leaven of the Pharisees and of the Sadducees.' Upon this text I wish to erect a beacon for all who desire to be saved, and to preserve some souls, if possible, from making shipwreck. The times call loudly for such beacons: the spiritual shipwrecks of the last twenty-five years have been deplorably numerous. The watchmen of the Church ought to speak out plainly now, or for ever hold their peace.

I. First of all, I ask my readers to observe *who they were to whom the warning of the text was addressed*.

Our Lord Jesus Christ was not speaking to men who were worldly, ungodly, and unsanctified, but to His own disciples, companions, and friends. He addressed men who, with the exception of the apostate Judas Iscariot, were right-hearted in the sight of God. He spoke to the twelve Apostles, the first founders of the Church of Christ, and the first ministers of the Word of salvation. And yet even to them He addressed the solemn caution of our text: 'Take heed and beware.'

There is something very remarkable in this fact. We might have thought that these Apostles needed little warning of this kind. Had they not given up all for Christ's sake? They had. – Had they not endured hardship for Christ's sake? They had. – Had they not believed Jesus, followed Jesus, loved Jesus, when almost all the world was unbelieving? All these things are true; and yet to them the caution was addressed: 'Take heed and beware.' We might have imagined that at any rate the disciples had but little to fear from the 'leaven of the Pharisees and of the Sadducees.' They were poor and unlearned men, most of them fishermen or publicans; they had no leanings in favour of the Pharisees and the Sadducees; they were more likely to be prejudiced against them than to feel any drawing towards them. All this is perfectly true; yet even to them there comes the solemn warning: 'Take heed and beware.'

There is useful counsel here for all who profess to love the Lord Jesus Christ in sincerity. It tells us loudly that the most eminent servants of Christ are not beyond the need of warnings, and ought to be always on their guard. It shows us plainly that the holiest of believers ought to walk humbly with his God, and to watch and pray, lest he fall into temptation, and be overtaken in a fault. None is so holy, but that he may fall, – not finally, not hopelessly, but to his own discomfort, to the scandal of the Church, and to the triumph of the world: none is so strong but that he may for a time be overcome. Chosen as believers are by God the Father, justified as they are by the blood and righteousness of Jesus Christ, sanctified as they are by the Holy Ghost, – believers are still only men: they are yet in the body, and yet in the world. They are ever near temptation: they are ever liable to err, both in doctrine and in practice. Their hearts, though renewed, are very feeble; their understanding, though enlightened, is still very dim. They ought to live like those who dwell in an enemy's land, and every day to put on the armour of God. The devil is very busy: he never slumbers or sleeps. Let us remember the falls of Noah, and Abraham, and Lot, and Moses, and David, and Peter; and remembering them, be humble, and take heed lest we fall.

I may be allowed to say that none need warnings so much as the ministers of Christ's Gospel. Our office and our ordination are no security against errors and mistakes. It is, alas, too true, that the greatest heresies have crept into the Church of Christ by means of ordained men. Neither Episcopal ordination, nor Presbyterian ordination, nor any other ordination, confers any immunity from error and false doctrine. Our very familiarity with the Gospel often begets in us a hardened state of mind. We are apt to read the Scriptures, and preach the Word, and conduct public worship, and carry on the service of God, in a dry, hard, formal, callous spirit. Our very familiarity with sacred things, except we watch our hearts, is likely to lead us astray. 'Nowhere,' says an old writer, 'is a man's soul in more danger than in a priest's office.' The history of the Church of Christ contains many melancholy proofs that the most distinguished ministers may for a time fall away. Who has not heard of Archbishop Cranmer recanting and going back from those opinions he had defended so stoutly, though, by God's mercy, raised again to witness a glorious confession at last? Who has not heard of Bishop Jewell signing documents that he most thoroughly disapproved, and of which signature he afterwards bitterly repented? Who does not know that many others might be named, who at one time or another, have been overtaken by faults, have fallen into errors, and been led astray? And who does not know the mournful fact that many of them never came back to the truth, but died in hardness of heart, and held their errors to the last?

These things ought to make us humble and cautious. They tell us to distrust our own hearts and to pray to be kept from falling. In these days, when we are specially called upon to cleave firmly to the doctrines of the Protestant Reformation, let us take heed that our zeal for Protestantism does not puff us up, and make us proud. Let us never say in our self-conceit, 'I shall never fall into Popery or Neologianism: those views will never suit me.' Let us remember that many have begun well and run well for a season, and yet afterwards turned aside out of the right way. Let us take heed that we are spiritual men as well as Protestants, and real friends of Christ as well as enemies of anti-Christ. Let us pray that we may be kept from error, and never forget that the twelve Apostles themselves were the men to whom the Great Head of the Church addressed these words: 'Take heed and beware.'

II. I propose, in the second place, to explain *what were those dangers against which our Lord warned the Apostles.* 'Take heed,' He says, 'and beware of the leaven of the Pharisees and of the Sadducees.'

The danger against which He warns them is false doctrine. He says nothing about the sword of persecution, or the open breach of the ten commandments, or the love of money, or the love of pleasure. All these things no doubt were perils and snares to which the souls of the Apostles were exposed; but against these things our Lord raises no warning voice here. His warning is confined to one single point: 'The leaven of the Pharisees and of the Sadducees.' – We are not left to conjecture what our Lord meant by that word 'leaven.' The Holy Ghost, a few verses after the very text on which I am now dwelling, tells us plainly that by leaven was meant the 'doctrine' of the Pharisees and of the Sadducees.

Let us try to understand what we mean when we speak of the 'doctrine of the Pharisees and of the Sadducees.'

(*a*) The doctrine of the Pharisees may be summed up in three words, – they were formalists, tradition-worshippers, and self-righteous. They attached such weight to the traditions of men that they practically regarded them of more importance than the inspired writings of the Old Testament. They valued themselves upon excessive strictness in their attention to all the ceremonial requirements of the Mosaic law. They thought much of being descended from

Abraham, and said in their hearts, 'We have Abraham for our father.' They fancied because they had Abraham for their father that they were not in peril of hell like other men, and that their descent from him was a kind of title to heaven. They attached great value to washings and ceremonial purifyings of the body, and believed that the very touching of the dead body of a fly or gnat would defile them. They made a great ado about the outward parts of religion, and such things as could be seen of men. They made broad their phylacteries, and enlarged the fringes of their garments. They prided themselves on paying great honour to dead saints, and garnishing the sepulchres of the righteous. They were very zealous to make proselytes. They thought much of having power, rank, and preeminence, and of being called by men, 'Rabbi, Rabbi.' These things, and many such-like things, the Phariseees did. Every well-informed Christian can find these things in the Gospels of St. Matthew and St. Mark. (See Matt. 15 and 23; Mark 7.)

All this time, be it remembered, they did not formally deny any part of the Old Testament Scripture. But they brought in, over and above it, so much of human invention, that they virtually put Scripture aside, and buried it under their own traditions. This is the sort of religion, of which our Lord says to the Apostles, 'Take heed and beware.'

(*b*) The doctrine of the Sadducees, on the other hand, may be summed up in three words, – free-thinking, scepticism, and rationalism. Their creed was one far less popular than that of the Pharisees, and, therefore, we find them less often mentioned in the New Testament Scriptures. So far as we can judge from the New Testament, they appear to have held the doctrine of degrees of inspiration; at all events they attached exceeding value to the Pentateuch above the other parts of the Old Testament, if indeed they did not altogether ignore the latter. They believed that there was no resurrection, no angel, and no spirit, and tried to laugh men out of their belief in these things, by supposing hard cases, and bringing forward difficult questions. We have an instance of their mode of argument in the case which they propounded to our Lord of the woman who had had seven husbands, when they asked, 'In the resurrection, whose wife shall she be of the seven?' And in this way they probably hoped, by rendering religion absurd, and its chief doctrines ridiculous, to make men altogether give up the faith they had received from the Scriptures.

All this time, be it remembered, we may not say that the Sadducees were downright infidels: this they were not. We may not say they denied revelation altogether: this they did not do. They observed the law of Moses. Many of them were found among the priests in the times described in the Acts of the Apostles. Caiaphas who condemned our Lord was a Sadducee. But the practical effect of their teaching was to shake men's faith in any revelation, and to throw a cloud of doubt over men's minds, which was only one degree better than infidelity. And of all such kind of doctrine, – free thinking, scepticism, rationalism, – our Lord says, 'Take heed and beware.'

Now the question arises, Why did our Lord Jesus Christ deliver this warning? He knew, no doubt, that within forty years the schools of the Pharisees and the Sadducees would be completely overthrown. He that knew all things from the beginning, knew perfectly well that in forty years Jerusalem, with its magnificent temple, would be destroyed, and the Jews scattered over the face of the earth. Why then do we find Him giving this warning about 'the leaven of the Pharisees and of the Sadducees'?

I believe that our Lord delivered this solemn warning for the perpetual benefit of that Church which He came on earth to found. He spoke with a prophetic knowledge. He knew well the diseases to which human nature is always liable. He foresaw that the two great plagues of His Church upon earth would always be the doctrine of the Pharisees and the doctrine of the Sadducees. He knew that these would be the upper and nether mill stones, between which His truth would be perpetually crushed and bruised until He came the second time. He knew that there always would be Pharisees in spirit, and Sadducees in spirit, among professing Christians. He knew that their succession would never fail, and their generation never become extinct, – and that though the names of Pharisees and Sadducees were no more, yet their principles would always exist. He knew that during the time that the Church existed, until His return, there would always be some that would add to the Word, and some that would subtract from it, – some that would stifle it, by adding to it other things, and some that would bleed it to death, by subtracting from its principal truths. And this is the reason why we find Him delivering this solemn warning: 'Take heed and beware of the leaven of the Pharisees and of the Sadducees.'

And now comes the question, Had not our Lord Jesus Christ good reason to give this warning? I appeal to all who know anything of Church history, Was there not indeed a cause? I appeal to all who remember what took place soon after the apostles were dead. Do we not read that in the primitive Church of Christ, there rose up two distinct parties; one ever inclined to err, like the Arians, in holding less than the truth, – the other ever inclined to err, like the relic worshippers and saint worshippers, in holding more than the truth as it is in Jesus? – Do we not see the same thing coming out in after times, in the form of Romanism on the one side and Socinianism on the other? – Do we not read in the history of our own Church of two great parties, the Non-jurors on the one side, and the Latitudinarians on the other? – These are ancient things. – In a short paper like this it is impossible for me to enter more fully into them. They are things well known to all who are familiar with records of past days. There always have been these two great parties, – the party representing the principles of the Pharisee, and the party representing the principles of the Sadducee. – And therefore our Lord had good cause to say of these two great principles, 'Take heed and beware.'

But, I desire to bring the subject even nearer at the present moment. I ask my readers to consider whether warnings like this are not especially needed in our own times. We have, undoubtedly, much to be thankful for in England. We have made great advances in arts and sciences in the last three centuries, and have much of the form and show of morality and religion. But, I ask anybody who can see beyond his own door, or his own fireside, whether we do not live in the midst of dangers from false doctrine?

We have amongst us, on the one side, a school of men who, wittingly or unwittingly, are paving the way into the Church of Rome, – a school that professes to draw its principles from primitive tradition, the writings of the Fathers, and the voice of the Church, – a school that talks and writes so much about the Church, the ministry, and the Sacraments, that it makes them like Aaron's rod, swallow up everything else in Christianity, – a school that attaches vast importance to the outward form and ceremonial of religion, – to gestures, postures, bowings, crosses, piscinas, sedilia, credence-tables, rood screens, albs, tunicles, copes, chasubles, altar cloths, incense, images, banners, processions, floral decorations, and many other like things, about which not a word is to be found in the Holy Scriptures as having any place in Christian worship. I refer, of course, to the school of Churchmen called Ritualists. When we examine the proceedings of that school, there can be but one conclusion concerning them. I believe whatever be the meaning and intention of its teachers, however devoted, zealous, and self-denying, many of them are, that upon them has fallen the mantle of the Pharisees.

We have, on the other hand, a school of men who, wittingly or unwittingly, appear to pave the way to Socinianism, – a school which holds strange views about the plenary inspiration of Holy Scripture, – stranger views about the doctrine of sacrifice, and the Atonement of our Lord and Saviour Jesus Christ, – strange views about the eternity of punishment, and God's love to man, – a school strong in negatives, but very weak in positives, – skilful in raising doubts, but impotent in laying them, – clever in unsettling and unscrewing men's faith, but powerless to offer any firm rest for the sole of our foot. And, whether the leaders of this school mean it or not, I believe that on them has fallen the mantle of the Sadducees.

These things sound harsh. It saves a vast deal of trouble to shut our eyes, and say, 'I see no danger,' and because it is not seen, therefore not to believe it. It is easy to stop our ears and say, 'I hear nothing,' and because we hear nothing, therefore to feel no alarm. But we know well who they are that rejoice over the state of things we have to deplore in some quarters of our own Church. We know what the Roman Catholic thinks: we know what the Socinian thinks. The Roman Catholic rejoices over the rise of the Tractarian party: the Socinian rejoices over the rise of men who teach such views as those set forth in modern days about the atonement and inspiration. They would not rejoice as they do if they did not see their work being done, and their cause being helped forward. The danger, I believe, is far greater than we are apt to suppose. The books that are read in many quarters are most mischievous, and the tone of thought on religious subjects, among many classes, and especially among the higher ranks, is deeply unsatisfactory. The plague is abroad. If we love life, we ought to search our own hearts, and try our own faith, and make sure that we stand on the right foundation. Above all, we ought to take heed that we ourselves do not imbibe the poison of false doctrine, and go back from our first love.

I feel deeply the painfulness of speaking out on these subjects. I know well that plain speaking about false doctrine is very unpopular, and that the speaker must be content to find himself thought very uncharitable, very troublesome, and very narrow-minded. Thousands of people can never distinguish differences in religion. To the bulk of men a clergyman is a clergyman, and a sermon is a sermon, and as to any difference between one minister and another, or one doctrine and another, they are utterly unable to understand it. I cannot expect such people to approve of any warning against false doctrine. I must make up my mind to meet with their disapprobation, and must bear it as I best can.

But I will ask any honest-minded, unprejudiced Bible reader to turn to the New Testament and see what he will find there. He will find many plain warnings against false doctrine: 'Beware of false prophets,' – 'Beware lest any man spoil you through philosophy and vain deceit,' – 'Be not carried about with divers and strange doctrines,' – 'Believe not every spirit, but try the spirits whether they be of God.' (Matt. 7:15; Col. 2:8; Heb. 13:9; 1 John 4:1). He will find a large part of several inspired epistles taken up with elaborate explanations of true doctrine and warnings against false teaching. I ask whether it is possible for a minister who takes the Bible for his rule of faith to avoid giving warnings against doctrinal error?

Finally, I ask any one to mark what is going on in England at this very day. I ask whether it is not true that hundreds have left the Established Church and joined the Church of Rome within the last thirty years? I ask whether it is not true that hundreds remain within our pale, who in heart are little better than Romanists, and who ought, if they were consistent, to walk in the steps of Newman and Manning, and go to their own place? – I ask again whether it is not true that scores of young men, both at Oxford and Cambridge, are spoiled and ruined by the withering influence of scepticism, and have lost all positive principles in religion? Sneers at religious newspapers, loud declarations of dislike to 'parties,' high-sounding, vague phrases about 'deep thinking, broad views, new light, free handling of Scripture, and the effete weakness of certain schools of theology,' make up the whole Christianity of many of the rising generation. – And yet, in the face of these notorious facts, men cry out, 'Hold your peace about false doctrine. Let false doctrine alone!' I cannot hold my peace. Faith in the Word of God, love to the souls of men, the vows I took when I was ordained, alike constrain me to bear witness against the errors of the day. And I believe that the saying of our Lord is eminently a truth for the times: 'Beware of the leaven of the Pharisees and of the Sadducees.'

III. The third thing to which I wish to call attention is *the peculiar name by which our Lord Jesus Christ speaks of the doctrines of the Pharisees and of the Sadducees.*

The words which our Lord used were always the wisest and the best that could be used. He might have said, 'Take heed and beware of the doctrine, or of the teaching, or of the opinions of the Pharisees and of the Sadducees.' But He does not say so: He uses a word of a peculiar nature. – He says, 'Take heed and beware of the *leaven* of the Pharisees and of the Sadducees.'

Now we all know what is the true meaning of the word 'leaven.' It is what we commonly call yeast, – the yeast which is added to the lump of dough in making a loaf of bread. This yeast, or leaven, bears but a small proportion to the lump into which it is thrown; just so, our Lord would have us know, the first beginning of false doctrine is but small compared to the body of Christianity. – It works quietly and noiselessly; just so, our Lord would have us know, false doctrine works secretly in the heart in which it is once planted. – It insensibly changes the character of the whole mass with which it is mingled; just so, our Lord would have us know, the doctrines of the Pharisees and Sadducees turn everything upside down, when once admitted into a Church or into a man's heart. – Let us mark these points: they throw light on many things that we see in the present day. It is of vast importance to receive the lessons of wisdom that this word 'leaven' contains in itself.

False doctrine does not meet men face to face, and proclaim that it is false. It does not blow a trumpet before it, and endeavour openly to turn us away from the truth as it is in Jesus. It does not come before men in broad day, and summon them to surrender. It approaches us secretly, quietly, insidiously, plausibly, and in such a way as to disarm man's suspicion, and throw him off his guard. It is the wolf in sheep's clothing, and Satan in the garb of an angel of light, who have always proved the most dangerous foes of the Church of Christ.

I believe the most powerful champion of the Pharisees is not the man who bids you openly and honestly come out and join the Church of Rome: it is the man who says that he agrees on all points with you in *doctrine*. He would not take anything away from those evangelical views that you hold; – he would not have you make any change at all; – all he asks you to do is to *add* a little more to your belief, in order to make your Christianity perfect. 'Believe me,' he says, 'we do not want you to give up anything. We only want you to hold a few more clear views about the Church and the sacraments. We want you to add to your present opinions a little more about the office of the ministry, and a little more about episcopal authority, and a little more about the Prayer-book, and a little more about the necessity of order and of discipline. – We only want you to add *a little more* of these things to your system of religion, and you will be quite right.' But when men speak to you in this way, then is the time to remember what our Lord said, and to 'take heed and beware.' This is the leaven of the Pharisees, against which we are to stand upon our guard.

Why do I say this? I say it because there is no security against the doctrine of the Pharisees, unless we resist its principles in their beginnings. Beginning with a 'little more about the Church,' you may one day place the Church in the room of Christ. – Beginning with a 'little more about the ministry,' you may one day regard the minister as 'the mediator between God and man.' – Beginning with a 'little more about the sacraments,' you may one day altogether give up the doctrine of justification by faith without the deeds of the law. – Beginning with a 'little more reverence for the Prayer-book,' you may one day place it above the holy Word of God Himself. – Beginning with a 'little more honour to Bishops,' you may at last refuse salvation to every one who does not belong to an Episcopal Church. – I only tell an old story: I only mark out roads that have been trodden by hundreds of members of the Church of England in the last few years. They began by carping at the Reformers, and have ended by swallowing the decrees of the Council of Trent. They began by crying up Laud and the non-jurors, and have ended by going far beyond them, and formally joining the Church of Rome. I believe that when we hear men asking us to 'add a little more' to our good old plain Evangelical views, we should stand upon our guard. We should remember our Lord's caution: 'Of the leaven of the Pharisees take heed and beware.'

I consider the most dangerous champion of the Sadducee school is not the man who tells you openly that he wants you to lay aside any part of the truth, and to become a free-thinker and a sceptic. It is the man who begins with quietly insinuating doubts as to the position that we ought to take up about religion, – doubts whether we ought to be so positive in saying 'this is truth, and that falsehood,' – doubts whether we ought to think men wrong who differ from us on religious opinions, since they *may* after all be as much right as we are. – It is the man who tells us we ought not to condemn anybody's views, lest we err on the side of want of charity. – It is the man who always begins talking in a vague way about God being a God of love, and hints that we ought to believe perhaps that all men, whatever doctrine they profess, will be saved. – It is the man who is ever reminding us that we ought to take care how we think lightly of men of powerful minds, and great intellects (*though they are deists and sceptics*), who do not think as we do, and that, after all, 'great minds are all more or less, taught of God!' – It is the man who is ever harping on the difficulties of inspiration, and raising questions whether all men may not be found saved in the end, and whether all may not be right in the sight of God. – It is the man who crowns this kind of talk by a few calm sneers against what he is pleased to call 'old-fashioned views,' and 'narrow-minded theology,' and 'bigotry,' and the 'want of liberality and charity,' in the present day. But when men begin to speak to us in this kind of way, then is the time to stand upon our guard. Then is the time to remember the words of our Lord Jesus Christ, and 'to take heed and beware of leaven.'

Once more, why do I say this? I say it because there is no security against Saduceeism, any more than against Phariseeism, unless we resist its principles in the bud. Beginning with a little vague talk about 'charity,' you may end in the doctrine of universal salvation, fill heaven with a mixed multitude of wicked as well as good, and deny the existence of hell. – Beginning with a few high-sounding phrases about intellect and the inner light in man, you may end with denying the work of the Holy Ghost, and maintaining that Homer and Shakespeare were as truly inspired as St. Paul, and thus practically casting aside the Bible. – Beginning with some dreamy, misty idea about 'all religions containing more or less truth,' you may end with utterly denying the necessity of missions, and maintaining that the best plan is to leave everybody alone. – Beginning with dislike to 'Evangelical religion,' as old-fashioned, narrow, and exclusive, you may end by rejecting every leading doctrine of Christianity, – the atonement, the need of grace, and the divinity of Christ. Again I repeat that I only tell an old story: I only give a sketch of a path which scores have trodden in the last few years. They were once satisfied with such divinity as that of Newton, Scott, Cecil, and Romaine; they are now fancying they have found a more excellent way in the principles which have been propounded by theologians of the Broad school! I believe there is no safety for a man's soul unless he remembers the lesson involved in those solemn words, 'Beware of the leaven of the Sadducees.'

Let us beware of the *insidiousness* of false doctrine. Like the fruit of which Eve and Adam ate, it looks at first sight pleasant and good, and a thing to be desired. Poison is not written upon it, and so people are not afraid. Like counterfeit coin, it is not stamped 'bad:' it passes current from the very likeness it bears to the truth.

Let us beware of the *very small beginnings* of false doctrine. Every heresy began at one time with some little departure from the truth. There is only a little seed of error needed to create a great tree. It is the little stones that make up the mighty building. It was the little timbers that made the great ark that carried Noah and his family over a deluged world. It is the little leaven that leavens the whole lump. It is the little flaw in one link of the chain cable that wrecks the gallant ship, and drowns the crew. It is the omission or addition of one little item in the doctor's prescription that spoils the whole medicine, and turns it into poison. We do not tolerate quietly a little dishonesty, or a little cheating, or a little lying: just so, let us never allow a little false doctrine to ruin us, by thinking it is but a 'little one,' and can do no harm. The Galatians seemed to be doing nothing very dangerous when they 'observed days and months, and times and years;' yet St. Paul says, 'I am afraid of you.' (Gal. 4 : 10, 11.)

Finally, let us beware of supposing that *we at any rate are not in danger.* 'Our views are sound : our feet stand firm : others may fall away, but we are safe!' Hundreds have thought the same, and have come to a bad end. In their self-confidence they tampered with little temptations and little forms of false doctrine; in their self-conceit they went near the brink of danger; and now they seem lost for ever. They appear given over to a strong delusion, so as to believe a lie. Some of them have exchanged the Prayer-book for the Breviary, and are praying to the Virgin Mary, and bowing down to images. Others of them are casting overboard one doctrine after another, and bid fair to strip themselves of every sort of religion but a few scraps of Deism. Very striking is the vision in Pilgrim's Progress, which describes the hill Error as 'very steep on the farthest side;' and 'when Christian and Hopeful looked down they saw at the bottom several men dashed all to pieces by a fall they had from the top.' – Never, never let us forget the caution to beware of 'leaven;' and if we think we stand, let us 'take heed lest we fall.'

IV. I propose in the fourth and last place, to suggest *some safeguards and antidotes against the dangers of the present day, – the leaven of the Pharisees and the leaven of the Sadducees.*

I feel that we all need more and more the presence of the Holy Ghost in our hearts, to guide, to teach, and to keep us sound in the faith. We all need to watch more, and to pray to be held up, and preserved from falling away. But still, there are certain great truths, which, in a day like this, we are specially bound to keep in mind. There are times when some common epidemic invades a land, when medicines, at all times valuable, become of peculiar value. There are places where a peculiar malaria prevails, in which remedies, in every place valuable, are more than ever valuable in consequence of it. So I believe there are times and seasons in the Church of Christ when we are bound to tighten our hold upon certain great leading truths, to grasp them with more than ordinary firmness in our hands, to press them to our hearts, and not to let them go. Such doctrines I desire to set forth in order, as the great antidotes to the leaven of the Pharisees and of the Sadducees. When Saul and Jonathan were slain by the archers, David ordered the children of Israel to be taught the use of the bow.

(a) For one thing, if we would be kept sound in the faith, we must take heed to our doctrine about the *total corruption of human nature*. The corruption of human nature is no slight thing. It is no partial, skin-deep disease, but a radical and universal corruption of man's will, intellect, affections, and conscience. We are not merely poor and pitiable sinners in God's sight: we are guilty sinners; we are blameworthy sinners: we deserve justly God's wrath and God's condemnation. I believe there are very few errors and false doctrines of which the beginning may not be traced up to unsound views about the corruption of human nature. Wrong views of a disease will always bring with them wrong views of the remedy. Wrong views of the corruption of human nature will always carry with them wrong views of the grand antidote and cure of that corruption.

(*b*) For another thing, we must take heed to our doctrine about *the inspiration and authority of the Holy Scriptures*. Let us boldly maintain, in the face of all gainsayers, that the whole of the Bible is given by inspiration of the Holy Ghost, – that all is inspired completely, not one part more than another, – and that there is an entire gulf between the Word of God and any other book in the world. – We need not be afraid of difficulties in the way of the doctrine of plenary inspiration. There may be many things about it far too high for us to comprehend: it is a miracle, and all miracles are necessarily mysterious. But if we are not to believe anything until we can entirely explain it, there are very few things indeed that we shall believe. – We need not be afraid of all the assaults that criticism brings to bear upon the Bible. From the days of the apostles the Word of the Lord has been incessantly 'tried,' and has never failed to come forth as gold, uninjured, and unsullied. – We need not be afraid of the discoveries of science. Astronomers may sweep the heavens with telescopes, and geologists may dig down into the heart of the earth, and never shake the authority of the Bible: 'The voice of God, and the work of God's hands never will be found to contradict one another.' – We need not be afraid of the researches of travellers. They will never discover anything that contradicts God's Bible. I believe that if a Layard were to go over all the earth and dig up a hundred buried Ninevehs, there would not be found a single inscription which would contradict a single fact in the Word of God.

Furthermore, we must boldly maintain that this Word of God is the only rule of faith and of practice, – that whatsoever is not written in it cannot be required of any man as needful to salvation, – and that however plausibly new doctrines may be defended, if they be not in the Word of

[63]

God they cannot be worth our attention. It matters nothing who says a thing, whether he be bishop, archdeacon, dean, or presbyter. It matters nothing that the thing is well said, eloquently, attractively, forcibly, and in such a way as to turn the laugh against you. We are not to believe it except it be proved to us by Holy Scripture.

Last, but not least, we must use the Bible as if we believed it was given by inspiration. We must use it with reverence, and read it with all the tenderness with which we would read the words of an absent father. We must not expect to find in a book inspired by the Spirit of God no mysteries. We must rather remember that in nature there are many things we cannot understand; and that as it is in the book of nature, so it will always be in the book of Revelation. We should draw near to the Word of God in that spirit of piety recommended by Lord Bacon many years ago. 'Remember,' he says, speaking of the book of nature, 'that man is not the master of that book, but the interpreter of that book.' And as we deal with the book of nature, so we must deal with the Book of God. We must draw near to it, not to teach, but to learn, – not like the master of it but like a humble scholar, seeking to understand it.

(c) For another thing, we must take heed to our doctrine respecting *the atonement and priestly office of our Lord and Saviour Jesus Christ*. We must boldly maintain that the death of our Lord upon the cross was no common death. It was not the death of one who only died like Cranmer, Ridley, and Latimer, as a martyr. It was not the death of one who only died to give us a mighty example of self-sacrifice and self-denial. The death of Christ was an offering up unto God of Christ's own body and blood, to make satisfaction for man's sin and transgression. It was a sacrifice and propitiation; a sacrifice typified in every offering of the Mosaic law, a sacrifice of the mightiest influence upon all mankind. Without the shedding of that blood there could not be, – there never was to be, – any remission of sin.

Furthermore, we must boldly maintain that this crucified Saviour ever sitteth at the right hand of God, to make intercession for all that come to God by Him; that He there represents and pleads for them that put their trust in Him; and that He has deputed His office of Priest and Mediator to no man, or set of men on the face of the earth. We need none besides. We need no Virgin Mary, no angels, no saint, no priest, no person ordained or unordained, to stand between us and God, but the one Mediator, Christ Jesus.

Furthermore, we must boldly maintain that peace of conscience is not to be bought by confession to a priest, and by receiving a man's absolution from sin. It is to be had only by going to the great High Priest, Christ Jesus; by confession before Him, not before man; and by absolution from Him only, who alone can say, 'Thy sins be forgiven thee: go in peace.'

Last, but not least, we must boldly maintain that peace with God, once obtained by faith in Christ, is to be kept up, not by mere outward ceremonial acts of worship, – not by receiving the sacrament of the Lord's Supper every day, – but by the daily habit of looking to the Lord Jesus Christ by faith, – eating by faith His body, and drinking by faith His blood; that eating and drinking of which our Lord says that he who eats and drinks shall find His 'body meat indeed, and His blood drink indeed.' Holy John Owen declared, long ago, that if there was any one point more than another that Satan wished to overthrow, it was the Priestly office of our Lord and Saviour Jesus Christ. Satan knew well, he said, that it was the 'principal foundation of faith and consolation of the Church.' Right views upon that office are of essential importance in the present day, if men would not fall into error.

(*d*) One more remedy I must mention. We must take heed to our doctrine about *the work of God the Holy Ghost*. Let us settle it in our minds that His work is no uncertain invisible operation upon the heart: and that where He is, He is not hidden, not unfelt, not unobserved. We do not believe that the dew, when it falls, cannot be felt, or that where there is life in a man it cannot be seen and observed by his breath. So is it with the influence of the Holy Ghost. No man has any right to lay claim to it, except its fruits, – its experimental effects, – can be seen in his life. Where He is, there will ever be a new creation, and a new man. Where He is, there will ever be new knowledge, new faith, new holiness, new fruits in the life, in the family, in the world, in the Church. And where these new things are not to be seen we may well say, with confidence, there is no work of the Holy Ghost. These are times in which we all need to be upon our guard about the doctrine of the work of the Spirit. Madame Guyon said, long ago, that the time would perhaps come when men might have to be martyrs for the work of the Holy Ghost. That time seems not far distant. At any rate, if there is one truth in religion that seems to have more contempt showered upon it than another, it is the work of the Spirit.

I desire to impress the immense importance of these four points upon all who read this paper: (*a*) clear views of the sinfulness of human nature; (*b*) clear views of the inspiration of Scripture; (*c*) clear views of the Atonement and Priestly office of our Lord and Saviour Jesus Christ; (*d*) and clear views of the work of the Holy Ghost. I believe that strange doctrines about the Church, the ministry, and the Sacraments, – about the love of God, the death of Christ, and the eternity of punishment, – will find no foothold in the heart which is sound on these four points. I believe that they are four great safeguards against the leaven of the Pharisees and of the Sadducees.

I will now conclude this paper with a few remarks by way of practical application. My desire is to make the whole subject useful to those into whose hands these pages may fall, and to supply an answer to the questions which may possibly arise in some hearts, – What are we to do? What advice have you got to offer for the times?

(1) In the first place, I will ask every reader of this paper to find out whether he has *saving personal religion for his own soul*. This is the principal thing after all. It will profit no man to belong to a sound visible Church, if he does not himself belong to Christ. It will avail a man nothing to be intellectually sound in the faith, and to approve sound doctrine, if he is not himself sound at heart. Is this the case with you? Can you say that your heart is right in the sight of God? Is it renewed by the Holy Ghost? Does Christ dwell in it by faith? O, rest not, rest not, till you can give a satisfactory answer to these questions! The man who dies unconverted, however sound his views, is as truly lost for ever as the worst Pharisee or Sadducee that ever lived.

(2) In the next place, let me beseech every reader of this paper who desires to be sound in the faith, to *study diligently the Bible*. That blessed book is given to be a light to our feet, and a lantern to our path. No man who reads it reverently, prayerfully, humbly, and regularly, shall ever be allowed to miss the way to heaven. By it every sermon,

and every religious book, and every ministry ought to be weighed and proved. Would you know what is truth? Do you feel confused and puzzled by the war of words which you hear on every side about religion? Do you want to know what you ought to believe, and what you ought to be and do, in order to be saved? Take down your Bible, and cease from man. Read your Bible with earnest prayer for the teaching of the Holy Ghost; read it with honest determination to abide by its lessons. Do so steadily and perseveringly, and you shall see light: you shall be kept from the leaven of the Pharisees and Sadducees, and be guided to eternal life. The way to do a thing is to do it. Act upon this advice without delay.

(3) In the next place, let me advise every reader of this paper who has reason to hope that he is sound in faith and heart, to *take heed to the proportion of truths*. I mean by that to impress the importance of giving each several truth of Christianity the same place and position in our hearts which is given to it in God's Word. The first things must not be put second, and the second things must not be put first in our religion. The Church must not be put above Christ; the sacraments must not be put above faith and the work of the Holy Ghost. Ministers must not be exalted above the place assigned to them by Christ; means of grace must not be regarded as an end instead of a means. Attention to this point is of great moment: the mistakes which arise from neglecting it are neither few nor small. Here lies the immense importance of studying the whole Word of God, omitting nothing, and avoiding partiality in reading one part more than another. Here again lies the value of having a clear system of Christianity in our minds. Well would it be for the Church of England if all its members read the thirty-nine Articles, and marked the beautiful

order in which those Articles state the main truths which men ought to believe.

(4) In the next place, let me entreat every true hearted servant of Christ *not to be deceived by the specious guise* under which false doctrines often approach our souls in the present day. Beware of supposing that a teacher of religion is to be trusted, because although he holds some unsound views, he yet 'teaches a great deal of truth.' Such a teacher is precisely the man to do you harm: poison is always most dangerous when it is given in small doses and mixed with wholesome food. Beware of being taken in by the apparent earnestness of many of the teachers and upholders of false doctrine. Remember that zeal and sincerity and fervour are no proof whatever that a man is working for Christ, and ought to be believed. Peter no doubt was in earnest when he bade our Lord spare Himself, and not go to the cross; yet our Lord said to him, 'Get thee behind Me, Satan.' Saul no doubt was in earnest when he went to and fro persecuting Christians; yet he did it ignorantly, and his zeal was not according to knowledge. The founders of the Spanish Inquisition no doubt were in earnest, and in burning God's saints alive thought they were doing God service; yet they were actually persecuting Christ's members and walking in the steps of Cain. – It is an awful fact that, 'Satan himself is transformed into an angel of light.' (2 Cor. 11 : 14.) Of all the delusions prevalent in these latter days, there is none greater than the common notion that 'if a man is in earnest about his religion he must be a good man!' Beware of being carried away by this delusion; beware of being led astray by 'earnest-minded men!' Earnestness is in itself an excellent thing; but it must be earnestness in behalf of Christ and His whole truth, or else it is worth

nothing at all. The things that are highly esteemed among men are often abominable in the sight of God.

(5) In the next place, let me counsel every true servant of Christ to *examine his own heart* frequently and carefully as to his state before God. This is a practice which is useful at all times: it is specially desirable at the present day. When the great plague of London was at its height people remarked the least symptoms that appeared on their bodies in a way that they never remarked them before. A spot here, or a spot there, which in time of health men thought nothing of, received close attention when the plague was decimating families, and striking down one after another! So ought it to be with ourselves, in the times in which we live. We ought to watch our hearts with double watchfulness. We ought to give more time to meditation, self-examination, and reflection. It is a hurrying, bustling age: if we would be kept from falling, we must make time for being frequently alone with God.

(6) Last of all, let me urge all true believers *to contend earnestly for the faith once delivered to the saints*. We have no cause to be ashamed of that faith. I am firmly persuaded that there is no system so life-giving, so calculated to awaken the sleeping, lead on the inquiring, and build up the saints, as that system which is called the *Evangelical* system of Christianity. Wherever it is faithfully preached, and efficiently carried out, and consistently adorned by the lives of its professors, it is the power of God. It may be spoken against and mocked by some; but so it was in the days of the Apostles. It may be weakly set forth and defended by many of its advocates; but, after all, its fruits and its results are its highest praise. No other system of religion can point to such fruits. Nowhere are so many souls converted to God as in those congregations where the

Gospel of Jesus Christ is preached in all its fulness, without any admixture of the Pharisee or Sadducee doctrine. We are not called upon, beyond all doubt, to be nothing but controversialists; but we never ought to be ashamed to testify to the truth as it is in Jesus, and to stand up boldly for Evangelical religion. We have the truth, and we need not be afraid to say so. The judgment-day will prove who is right, and to that day we may boldly appeal.

5: Divers and Strange Doctrines

*'Be not carried about with divers and strange doctrines.
For it is a good thing that the heart be established
with grace; not with meats, which have not
profited them that have been occupied
therein' (Heb. 13:9).*

THE TEXT WHICH HEADS THIS PAPER IS AN APOS-
tolic caution against false doctrine. It forms part of a
warning which St. Paul addressed to Hebrew Christians.
It is a caution just as much needed now as it was eighteen
hundred years ago. Never, I think, was it so important for
Christian ministers to cry aloud continually, 'Be not carried
about.'

That old enemy of mankind, the devil, has no more
subtle device for ruining souls than that of spreading false
doctrine. 'A murderer and a liar from the beginning,' he
never ceases going to and fro in the earth, 'seeking whom
he may devour.' – Outside the Church he is ever persuad-
ing men to maintain barbarous customs and destructive
superstitions. Human sacrifice to idols, – gross revolting,
cruel, disgusting worship of abominable false deities, –
persecution, slavery, cannibalism, child murder, devastat-
ing religious wars, – all these are a part of Satan's handi-
work, and the fruit of his suggestions. Like a pirate, his
object is to 'sink, burn, and destroy.' – Inside the Church
he is ever labouring to sow heresies, to propagate errors,
to foster departures from the faith. If he cannot prevent
the waters flowing from the Fountain of Life, he tries hard
to poison them. If he cannot destroy the medicine of the
Gospel, he strives to adulterate and corrupt it. No wonder
that he is called 'Apollyon, the destroyer.'

The Divine Comforter of the Church, the Holy Ghost, has always employed one great agent to oppose Satan's devices. That agent is the Word of God. The Word expounded and unfolded, the Word explained and opened up, the Word made clear to the head and applied to the heart, – the Word is the chosen weapon by which the devil must be confronted and confounded. The Word was the sword which the Lord Jesus wielded in the temptation. To every assault of the Tempter, He replied, 'It is written.' The Word is the sword which His ministers must use in the present day, if they would successfully resist the devil. The Bible, faithfully and freely expounded, is the safeguard of Christ's Church.

I desire to remember this lesson, and to invite attention to the text which stands at the head of this paper. We live in an age when men profess to dislike dogmas and creeds, and are filled with a morbid dislike to controversial theology. He who dares to say of one doctrine that 'it is true,' and of another that 'it is false,' must expect to be called narrow-minded and uncharitable, and to lose the praise of men. Nevertheless, the Scripture was not written in vain. Let us examine the mighty lessons contained in St. Paul's words to the Hebrews. They are lessons for us as well as for them.

I. First, we have here a *broad warning:* 'Be not carried about with divers and strange doctrines.'

II. Secondly, we have here a *valuable prescription:* 'It is good that the heart be established with grace, not with meats.'

III. Lastly, we have here an *instructive fact:* 'Meats have not profited them which have been occupied therein.'

On each of these points I have somewhat to say. If we patiently plough up this field of truth, we shall find that there is precious treasure hidden in it.

I. First comes the *broad warning:* 'Be not carried about with divers and strange doctrines.'

The meaning of these words is not a hard thing which we cannot understand. 'Be not tossed to and fro,' the Apostle seems to say, 'by every blast of false teaching, like ships without compass or rudder. False doctrines will arise as long as the world lasts, in number many, in minor details varying, in one point alone always the same, – strange, new, foreign, and departing from the Gospel of Christ. They do exist now. They will always be found within the visible Church. Remember this, and be not carried away.' Such is St. Paul's warning.

The Apostle's warning does not stand alone. Even in the midst of the Sermon on the Mount there fell from the loving lips of our Saviour a solemn caution: 'Beware of false prophets, which come unto you in sheep's clothing, but inwardly they are ravening wolves.' (Matt. 7:15.) Even in St. Paul's last address to the Ephesian elders, though he finds no time to speak about the Sacraments, he does find time to warn his friends against false doctrine: 'Of your own selves shall men arise, speaking perverse things to draw away disciples after them.' (Acts 20:30.) What says the Second Epistle to the Corinthians: 'I fear, lest by any means, as the serpent beguiled Eve through his subtilty, so your minds should be corrupted from the simplicity that is in Christ.' (2 Cor. 11:3.) What says the Epistle to the Galatians: 'I marvel that ye are so soon removed from him that called you into the grace of Christ unto another Gospel.' – 'Who hath bewitched you that ye should not obey the truth?' – 'Having begun in the Spirit, are ye now made perfect by the flesh?' – 'How turn ye again to weak and beggarly elements?' – 'Ye observe days, and months, and times, and years. I am afraid of you.' – 'Stand fast in the liberty wherewith Christ hath made us free, and be not entangled again in the yoke of bondage.' (Gal. 1:6; 3:1, 3; 4:9, 10, 11; 5:1.) What says the Epistle to the Ephesians: 'Be no more children, tossed to and fro, and carried about with every wind of doctrine.' (Eph. 4:14.) What says the Epistle to the Colossians: 'Beware lest any man spoil you through philosophy and vain deceit, after the tradition of men.' (Col. 2:8.) What says the First Epistle to Timothy: 'The Spirit speaketh expressly, that in the latter times some shall depart from the faith.' (1 Tim. 4:1.) What says the Second Epistle of Peter: 'There shall be false teachers among you, who privily shall bring in damnable heresies.' (2 Peter 2:1.) What says the First Epistle of John: 'Believe not every spirit. Many false prophets are gone out into the world.' (1 John 4:1.) What says the Epistle of Jude: 'Contend earnestly for the faith once delivered to the saints. For there are certain men crept in unawares.' (Jude 1:3, 4.) Let us mark well these texts. These things were written for our learning.

What shall we say to these texts? How they may strike others I cannot say. I only know how they strike me. To tell us, as some do, in the face of these texts, that the early Churches were a model of perfection and purity, is absurd. Even in Apostolic days, its appears, there were abundant errors both in doctrine and practice. – To tell us, as others do, that clergymen ought never to handle controversial subjects, and never to warn their people against erroneous views, is senseless and unreasonable. At this rate we might neglect not a little of the New Testament. Surely the dumb dog and the sleeping shepherd are the best allies of the wolf, the thief, and the robber. It is not for nothing that St. Paul says, 'If thou put the brethren in remembrance of these things, thou shalt be a good minister of Jesus Christ.' (1 Tim. 4:5.)

A plain warning against false doctrine is specially needed in England in the present day. The school of the Pharisees, and the school of the Sadduceees, those ancient mothers of all mischief, were never more active than they are now. Between men adding to the truth on one side, and men taking away from it on the other, – between those who bury truth under additions, and those who mutilate it by subtractions, – between superstition and infidelity, – between Romanism and neology, – between Ritualism and Rationalism, – between these upper and nether millstones the Gospel is well nigh crushed to death!

Strange views are continually propounded by clergymen about subjects of the deepest importance. About the atonement, the divinity of Christ, the inspiration of the Bible, the reality of miracles, the eternity of future punishment, – about the Church, the ministerial office, the Sacraments, the confessional, the honour due to the Virgin, prayers for the dead, – about all these things there is nothing too monstrous to be taught by some English ministers in these latter days. By the pen and by the tongue, by the press and by the pulpit, the country is incessantly deluged with a flood of erroneous opinions. To ignore the fact is mere affectation. Others see it, if we pretend to be ignorant of it. The danger is real, great, and unmistakable. Never was it so needful to say, 'Be not carried about.'

Many things combine to make the present inroad of false doctrine peculiarly dangerous. There is an undeniable zeal in some of the teachers of error: their 'earnestness' (to

use an unhappy cant phrase) makes many think they must
be right. There is a great appearance of learning and theological knowledge: many fancy that such clever and intellectual men must surely be safe guides. There is a general
tendency to free thought and free inquiry in these latter
days: many like to prove their independence of judgment,
by believing novelties. There is a wide-spread desire to
appear charitable and liberal-minded: many seem half
ashamed of saying that anybody can be in the wrong. There
is a quantity of half-truth taught by the modern false
teachers: they are incessantly using Scriptural terms and
phrases in an unscriptural sense. There is a morbid craving
in the public mind for a more sensuous, ceremonial, sen-
sational, showy worship: men are impatient of inward,
invisible heart-work. There is a silly readiness in every
direction to believe everybody who talks cleverly, lovingly,
and earnestly, and a determination to forget that Satan is
often 'transformed into an angel of light.' (2 Cor. 2:14.)
There is a wide-spread 'gullibility' among professing
Christians: every heretic who tells his story plausibly is
sure to be believed, and everybody who doubts him is
called a persecutor and a narrow-minded man. All these
things are peculiar symptoms of our times. I defy any observing man to deny them. They tend to make the assaults
of false doctrine in our day peculiarly dangerous. They
make it more than ever needful to cry aloud, 'Be not
carried about.'

Does any one ask me, What is the best safeguard against
false doctrine? – I answer in one word, 'The Bible: the
Bible regularly read, regularly prayed over, regularly
studied.' We must go back to the old prescription of our
Master: 'Search the Scriptures.' (John 5:39.) If we want a
weapon to wield against the devices of Satan, there is noth-

ing like 'the sword of the Spirit, the Word of God.' But to wield it successfully, we must read it habitually, diligently, intelligently, and prayerfully. This is a point on which, I fear, many fail. In an age of hurry and bustle, few read their Bibles as much as they should. More books perhaps are read than ever, but less of the one Book which makes man wise unto salvation. Rome and neology could never have made such havoc in the Church in the last fifty years, if there had not been a most superficial knowledge of the Scriptures throughout the land. A Bible-reading laity is the strength of a Church.

'Search the Scriptures.' Mark how the Lord Jesus Christ and His Apostles continually refer to the Old Testament, as a document just as authoritative as the New. Mark how they quote texts from the Old Testament, as the voice of God, as if every word was given by inspiration. Mark how the greatest miracles in the Old Testament are all referred to in the New, as unquestioned and unquestionable facts. Mark how all the leading events in the Pentateuch are incessantly named as historical events, whose reality admits of no dispute. Mark how the atonement, and substitution, and sacrifice, run through the whole Bible from first to last, as essential doctrines of revelation. Mark how the resurrection of Christ, the greatest of all miracles, is proved by such an overwhelming mass of evidence, that he who disbelieves it may as well say he will believe no evidence at all. Mark all these things, and you will find it very hard to be a Rationalist! Great are the difficulties of infidelity: it requires more credulity to be an infidel than a Christian. But greater still are the difficulties of Rationalism. Free handling of Scripture – results of modern criticism, – broad and liberal theology, – all these are fine, swelling, high-sounding phrases, which please some minds, and look very grand at a distance. But the man who looks below the surface of things will soon find that there is no sure standing-ground between ultra-Rationalism and Atheism.

'Search the Scriptures.' Mark what a conspicuous absence there is in the New Testament of what may be called the Sacramental system, and the whole circle of Ritualistic theology. Mark how extremely little there is said about the effects of Baptism. Mark how very seldom the Lord's Supper is mentioned in the Epistles. Find, if you can, a single text in which New Testament ministers are called sacrificing priests, – or the Lord's Supper is called a sacrifice, – or private confession to ministers is recommended and practised. – Turn, if you can, to one single verse in which sacrificial vestments are named as desirable, – or in which lighted candles, and pots of flowers on the Lord's Table, – or processions, and incense, and flags, and banners, and turning to the east, and bowing down to the bread and wine, – or prayer to the Virgin Mary and the angels, – are sanctioned. Mark these things well, and you will find it very hard to be a Ritualist! You may find your authority for Ritualism in garbled quotations from the Fathers, – in long extracts from monkish, mystical, or Popish writers; but you certainly will not find it in the Bible. Between the plain Bible, honestly and fairly interpreted, and extreme Ritualism there is gulf which cannot be passed.

If we would not be carried about by 'divers and strange doctrines,' we must remember the words of our Lord Jesus Christ: 'Search the Scriptures.' Ignorance of the Bible is the root of all error. Knowledge of the Bible is the best antidote against modern heresies.

II. I now proceed to examine St. Paul's *valuable prescription:* 'It is good that the heart be established with grace; not with meats.'

There are two words in this prescription which require a little explanation. A right understanding of them is absolutely essential to a proper use of the Apostle's advice. One of these words is 'meats,' and the other is 'grace.'

To see the full force of the word 'meats' we must remember the immense importance attached by many Jewish Christians to the distinctions of the ceremonial law about food. The flesh of some animals and birds, according to Leviticus, might be eaten, and that of others might not be eaten. Some meats were, consequently, called 'clean,' and others were called 'unclean.' To eat certain kinds of flesh made a Jew ceremonially unholy before God, and no strict Jew would touch and eat such food on any account. – Now were these distinctions still to be kept up after Christ ascended into heaven, or were they done away by the Gospel? Were heathen converts under any obligation to attend to the ceremonial of the Levitical law about food? Were Jewish Christians obliged to be as strict about the meats they ate as they were before Christ died, and the veil of the temple was rent in twain? Was the ceremonial law about meats entirely done away, or was it not? Was the conscience of a believer in the Lord Jesus to be troubled with fear lest his food should defile him?

Questions like these appear to have formed one of the great subjects of controversy in the Apostolic times. As is often the case, they assumed a place entirely out of proportion to their real importance. The Apostle Paul found it needful to handle the subject in no less than three of his Epistles to the Churches. – 'Meat,' he says, 'commends us not to God.' – 'The kingdom of God is not meat and drink.' – 'Let no man judge you in meat and drink.' (1 Cor. 8:8; Rom. 14:17; Col. 2:16.) Nothing shows the fallen nature of man so clearly as the readiness of morbid and scrupulous consciences to turn trifles into serious things. At last the controversy seems to have spread so far and obtained such dimensions, that 'meats' became an expression to denote anything ceremonial added to the Gospel as a thing of primary importance, any Ritual trifle thrust out of its lawful place and magnified into an essential of religion. In this sense, I believe, the word must be taken in the text now before us. By 'meats' St. Paul means ceremonial observances, either wholly invented by man, or else built on Mosaic precepts which have been abrogated and superseded by the Gospel. It is an expression which was well understood in the Apostolic days.

The word 'grace,' on the other hand, seems to be employed as a comprehensive description of the whole Gospel of Jesus Christ. Of that glorious Gospel, grace is the main feature, – grace in the original scheme – grace in the execution – grace in the application to man's soul. Grace is the fountain of life from which our salvation flows. Grace is the agency through which our spiritual life is kept up. Are we justified? it is by grace. – Are we called? it is by grace. – Have we forgiveness? it is through the riches of grace. – Have we good hope? it is through grace. – Do we believe? it is through grace. – Are we elect? it is by the election of grace. – Are we saved? it is by grace. – Why should I say more? The time would fail me to exhibit fully the part that grace does in the whole work of redemption. No wonder that St. Paul says to the Romans, 'We are not under the law, but under grace;' and tells Titus, 'The grace of God,

which bringeth salvation, hath appeared unto all men.'
(Rom. 3:24: Gal. 1:15; Eph. 1:7; 2 Thess. 2:16; Acts
18:27; Rom. 1:15; Eph. 2:5; Rom. 6:15; Titus 2:11.)

Such are the two great principles which St. Paul puts in
strong contrast in the prescription we are now considering.
He places opposite to one another 'meats' and 'grace,' –
Ceremonialism and the Gospel – Ritualism and the free
love of God in Christ Jesus. And then he lays down the
great principle that it is by 'grace,' and 'not meats,' that
the heart must be established.

Now 'establishment of heart' is one of the great wants
of many professing Christians. Specially is it longed after
by those whose knowledge is imperfect, and whose conscience is half enlightened. Such persons often feel in themselves much indwelling sin, and at the same time see very
indistinctly God's remedy and Christ's fulness. Their faith
is feeble, their hope dim, and their consolations small. They
want to realize more sensible comfort. They fancy they
ought to feel more and see more. They are not at ease.
They cannot attain to joy and peace in believing. Whither
shall they turn? What shall set their consciences at rest?
Then comes the enemy of souls, and suggests some short-
cut road to establishment. He hints at the value of some
addition to the simple plan of the Gospel, some man-made
device, some exaggeration of a truth, some flesh-satisfying
invention, some improvement on the old path, and whis-
pers, 'Only use this, and you shall be established.' Plausible
offers flow in at the same time from every quarter, like
quack medicines. Each has its own patrons and advocates.
On every side the poor unstable soul hears invitations to
move in some particular direction, and then shall come
perfect establishment.

'Come to us,' says the Roman Catholic. 'Join the Catholic Church, the Church on the Rock, the one, true, holy Church; the Church that cannot err. Come to her bosom, and repose your soul on her protection. Come to us, and you will find establishment.'

'Come to us,' says the extreme Ritualist. 'You need higher and fuller views of the priesthood and the Sacraments, of the Real Presence in the Lord's Supper, of the soothing influence of daily service, daily masses, auricular confession, and priestly absolution. Come and take up sound Church views, and you will find establishment.'

'Come to us,' says the violent Liberationist. 'Cast off the trammels and fetters of established Churches. Come out from all alliance with the State. Enjoy religious liberty. Throw away forms and Prayer-books. Use our shibboleth. Join our party. Cast in your lot with us, and you will soon be established.'

'Come to us,' say the Plymouth Brethren. 'Shake off all the bondage of creeds and Churches and systems. We will soon show you higher, deeper, more exalting, more enlightened views of truth. Join the brethren, and you will soon be established.'

'Come to us,' says the Rationalist. 'Lay aside the old worn-out clothes of effete schemes of Christianity. Give your reason free scope and play. Begin a freer mode of handling Scripture. Be no more a slave to an ancient old-world book. Break your chains and you shall be established.'

Every experienced Christian knows well that such appeals are constantly made to unsettled minds in the present day? Who has not seen that, when boldly and confidently made, they produce a painful effect on some people? Who has not observed that they often beguile un-stable souls, and lead them into misery for years?

'What saith the Scripture?' This is the only sure guide. Hear what St. Paul says. Heart establishment is not to be obtained by joining this party or that. It comes 'by grace, and not by meats.' Other things have a 'show of wisdom' perhaps, and give a temporary satisfaction 'to the flesh.' (Col. 2:23). But they have no healing power about them in reality, and leave the unhappy man who trusts them nothing bettered, but rather worse.

A clearer knowledge of the Divine scheme of grace, its eternal purposes, its application to man by Christ's re-deeming work, – a firmer grasp of the doctrine of grace, of God's free love in Christ, of Christ's full and complete satisfaction for sin, of justification by simple faith, – a more intimate acquaintance with Christ the Giver and Fountain of grace, His offices, His sympathy, His power, – a more thorough experience of the inward work of grace in the heart, – this, this, this is the grand secret of heart-establishment. This is the old path of peace. This is the true panacea for restless consciences. It may seem at first too simple, too easy, too cheap, too commonplace, too plain. But all the wisdom of man will never show the heavy-laden a better road to heart-rest. Secret pride and self-righteousness, I fear, are too often the reason why this good old road is not used.

I believe there never was a time when it was more needful to uphold the old Apostolic prescription than it is in the present day. Never were there so many unestablished and unsettled Christians wandering about, and tossed to and fro, from want of knowledge. Never was it so im-portant for faithful ministers to set the trumpet to their mouths and proclaim everywhere, 'Grace, grace, grace, not meats, establishes the heart.'

From the days of the Apostles there have never been wanting quack spiritual doctors, who have professed to heal the wounds of conscience with man-made remedies. In our own beloved Church there have always been some who have in heart turned back to Egypt, and, not content with the simplicity of our worship, have hankered after the ceremonial fleshpots of the Church of Rome. Laud, of unhappy memory, did a little in this way; but his doings were nothing compared to those of some clergymen in the present day. To hear the Sacraments incessantly exalted, and preaching cried down, – to see the Lord's Supper turned into an idol under the specious pretext of making it more honourable, – to find plain Prayer-book worship overlaid with so many newfangled ornaments and ceremonies that its essentials are quite buried, – how common is all this! These things were once a pestilence that walked in darkness. They are now a destruction that wastes in noonday. They are the joy of our enemies, the sorrow of the Church's best children, the damage of English Christianity, the plague of our times. And to what may they all be traced? To neglect or forgetfulness of St. Paul's simple prescription: 'Grace, and not meats, establishes the heart.'

Let us take heed that in our own personal religion, grace is all. Let us have clear systematic views of the Gospel of the grace of God. Nothing else will do good in the hour of sickness, in the day of trial, on the bed of death, and in the swellings of Jordan. Christ dwelling in our hearts by faith, Christ's free grace the only foundation under the soles of our feet, – this alone will give peace. Once let in self, and forms, and man's inventions, as a necessary part of our religion, and we are on a quicksand. We may be amused, excited, or kept quiet for a time, like children with toys, by a religion of 'meats.' Such a religion has 'a show of wisdom.' But unless our religion be one in which 'grace' is all, we shall never feel established.

III. In the last place, I proceed to examine *the instructive fact* which St. Paul records. He says, 'Meats have not profited them that have been occupied therein.'

We have no means of knowing whether the Apostle, in using this language, referred to any particular Churches or individuals. Of course it is possible that he had in view the Judaizing Christians of Antioch and Galatia, – or the Ephesians of whom he speaks to Timothy in his pastoral Epistle, – or the Colossians who caused him so much inward conflict, – or the Hebrew believers in every Church, without exception. It seems to me far more probable, however, that he had no particular Church or Churches in view. I rather think that he makes a broad, general, sweeping statement about all who in any place had exalted ceremonial at the expense of the doctrines of 'grace.' And he makes a wide declaration about them all. They have got no good from their favourite notions. They have not been more inwardly happy, more outwardly holy, or more generally useful. Their religion has been most unprofitable to them. Man-made alterations of God's precious medicine for sinners, – man-made additions to Christ's glorious Gospel, – however speciously defended and plausibly supported, do no real good to those that adopt them. They confer no increased inward comfort; they bring no growth of real holiness: they give no enlarged usefulness to the Church and the world. Calmly, quietly, and mildly, but firmly, decidedly, and unflinchingly, the assertion is made,

'Meats have *not profited* them that have been occupied therein.'

The whole stream of Church history abundantly confirms the truth of the Apostle's position. Who has not heard of the hermits and ascetics of the early centuries? Who has not heard of the monks and nuns and recluses of the Romish Church in the middle ages? Who has not heard of the burning zeal, the devoted self-denial of Romanists like Xavier, and Ignatius Loyola? The earnestness, the fervour, the self-sacrifice of all these classes, are matters beyond dispute. But none who read carefully and intelligently the records of their lives, yea, some of the best of them, can fail to see that they had no solid peace or inward rest of soul. Their very feverish restlessness is enough to show that their consciences were not at ease. None can fail to see that, with all their furious zeal and self-denial, they never did much good to the world. They gathered round themselves admiring partisans. They left a high reputation for self-denial and sincerity. They made men wonder at them while they lived, and sometimes canonize them when they died. But they did nothing to *convert souls*. And what is the reason of this? They attached an overweening importance to man-made ritual and ceremonial, and made less than they ought to have done of the Gospel of the grace of God. Their principle was to make much of 'meats,' and little of 'grace.' Hence they verified the words of St. Paul, 'Meats do not profit them that are occupied therein.'

The very history of our own times bears a striking testimony to the truth of St. Paul's assertion. In the last twenty-five years some scores of clergymen have seceded from the Church of England, and joined the Church of Rome. They wanted more of what they called Catholic doctrine and Catholic ceremonial. They honestly acted up to their principles, and went over to Rome. They were not all weak, and illiterate, and second-rate, and inferior men; several of them were men of commanding talents, whose gifts would have won for them a high position in any profession. Yet what have they gained by the step they have taken? What profit have they found in leaving 'grace' for 'meats,' in exchanging Protestantism for Catholicism? Have they attained a higher standard of holiness? Have they procured for themselves a greater degree of usefulness? – Let one of themselves supply an answer. Mr. Ffoulkes, a leading man in the party, within the last few years has openly declared that the preaching of some of his fellow 'perverts' is not so powerful as it was when they were English Churchmen, and that the highest degree of holy living he has ever seen is not within the pale of Rome, but in the quiet parsonages and unpretending family-life of godly English clergymen! Intentionally or not intentionally, wittingly or unwittingly, meaning it or not meaning it, nothing can be more striking than the testimony Mr. Ffoulkes bears to the truth of the Apostle's assertion: 'Meats do not profit' even those who make much ado about them. The religious system which exalts ceremonial and man-made ritual does no real good to its adherents, compared to the simple old Gospel of the grace of God.

Let us turn now, for a few moments, to the other side of the picture, and see what 'grace' has done. Let us hear how profitable the doctrines of the Gospel have proved to those who have clung firmly to them, and have not tried to mend and improve and patch them up by adding, as essentials, the 'meats' of man-made ceremonial.

It was 'grace, and not meats,' that made Martin Luther do the work that he did in the world. The key to all his success was his constant declaration of justification by faith, without the deeds of the law. This was the truth which enabled him to break the chains of Rome, and let light into Europe.

It was 'grace, and not meats,' that made our English martyrs, Latimer and Hooper, exercise so mighty an influence in life, and shine so brightly in death. They saw clearly, and taught plainly, the true priesthood of Christ, and salvation only by grace. They honoured God's grace, and God put honour on them.

It was 'grace, and not meats,' that made Romaine and Venn, and their companions, turn the world upside down in England, one hundred years ago. In themselves they were not men of extraordinary learning or intellectual power. But they revived and brought out again the real pure doctrines of grace.

It was 'grace, and not meats,' that made Simeon and Bishop Daniel Wilson and Bickersteth such striking instruments of usefulness in the first half of the present century. God's free grace was the great truth on which they relied, and continually brought forward. For so doing God put honour on them. They made much of God's grace, and the God of grace made much of them.

The list of ministerial biographies tells a striking tale. Who are those who have shaken the world, and left their mark on their generation, and aroused consciences, and converted sinners, and edified saints? Not those who have made asceticism, and ceremonials, and sacraments, and services, and ordinances the main thing; but those who have made most of God's free grace! In a day of strife, and controversy, and doubt, and perplexity, men forget this. Facts are stubborn things. Let us look calmly at them, and be not moved by those who tell us that daily services, frequent communions, processions, incense, bowings, crossings, confessions, absolutions, and the like, are the secret of a prosperous Christianity. Let us look at plain facts. Facts in old history, and facts in modern days, facts in every part of England, support the assertion of St. Paul. The religion of 'meats' does 'not profit those that are occupied therein.' It is the religion of grace that brings inward peace, outward holiness, and general usefulness.

Let me wind up this paper with a few words of practical application. We are living in an age of peculiar religious danger. I am quite sure that the advice I am going to offer deserves serious attention.

(1) In the first place, *let us not be surprised* at the rise and progress of false doctrine. It is a thing as old as the old Apostles. It began before they died. They predicted that there would be plenty of it before the end of the world. It is wisely ordered of God for the testing of our grace, and to prove who has real faith. If there were no such thing as false doctrine or heresy upon earth, I should begin to think the Bible was not true.

(2) In the next place, let us make up our minds *to resist false doctrine,* and not to be carried away by fashion and bad example. Let us not flinch, because all around us, high and low, rich and poor, are swept away, like geese in a flood, before a torrent of semi-popery. Let us be firm and stand our ground.

Let us resist false doctrine, and contend earnestly for the faith once delivered to the saints. Let us not be ashamed of showing our colours and standing out for New

Testament truth. Let us not be stopped by the cuckoo cry of 'controversy.' The thief likes dogs that do not bark, and watchmen that give no alarm. The devil is a thief and a robber. If we hold our peace, and do not resist false doctrine, we please him and displease God.

(3) In the next place, let us try *to preserve* the Old Protestant principles of the Church of England, and to hand them down uninjured to our children's children. Let us not listen to those faint-hearted Churchmen who would have us forsake the ship, and desert the Church of England in her time of need.

The Church of England is worth fighting for. She has done good service in days gone by, and she may yet do more, if we can keep her free from Popery and infidelity. Once readmit and sanction the Popish mass and auricular confession, and the Church of England will be ruined. Then let us fight hard for the Church of England being kept a Protestant Church. Let us read our thirty-nine Articles every year with attention, and learn from these Articles what are real Church principles. Let us arm our memories with these Articles, and be able to quote them. Before the edge and point of these Articles, fairly interpreted, ultra-Ritualists and ultra-Rationalists can never stand.

(4) In the last place, *let us make sure work of our own personal salvation.* Let us seek to know and feel that we ourselves are 'saved.'

The day of controversy is always a day of spiritual peril. Men are apt to confound orthodoxy with conversion, and to fancy that they must go to heaven if they know how to answer Papists. Yet mere earnestness without knowledge, and mere head-knowledge of Protestantism, alike save none. Let us never forget this.

Let us not rest till we feel the blood of Christ sprinkled on our consciences, and have the witness of the Spirit within us that we are born again. This is reality. This is true religion. This will last. This will never fail us. It is the possession of grace in the heart, and not the intellectual knowledge of it, that profits and saves the soul.

6: The Fallibility of Ministers

'But when Peter was come to Antioch, I withstood him to the face, because he was to be blamed.

'For before that certain came from James, he did eat with the Gentiles: but when they were come, he withdrew and separated himself, fearing them which were of the circumcision.

'And the other Jews dissembled likewise with him; insomuch that Barnabas also was carried away with their dissimulation.

'But when I saw that they walked not uprightly according to the truth of the gospel, I said unto Peter before them all, If thou, being a Jew, livest after the manner of Gentiles, and not as do the Jews, why compellest thou the Gentiles to live as do the Jews?

'We who are Jews by nature, and not sinners of the Gentiles,

'Knowing that a man is not justified by the works of the law, but by the faith of Jesus Christ, even we have believed in Jesus Christ, that we might be justified by the faith of Christ, and not by the works of the law: for by the works of the law shall no flesh be justified' (Gal.2:11–16).

HAVE WE EVER CONSIDERED WHAT THE APOSTLE Peter once did at Antioch? It is a question that deserves serious consideration.

What the Apostle Peter did *at Rome* we are often told, although we have hardly a jot of authentic information about it. Roman Catholic writers furnish us with many stories about this. Legends, traditions, and fables abound on the subject. But unhappily for these writers, Scripture is utterly silent upon the point. There is nothing in Scripture to show that the Apostle Peter ever was at Rome at all!

But what did the Apostle Peter do *at Antioch*? This is the point to which I want to direct attention. This is the subject from the passage from the Epistle to the Galatians, which heads this paper. On this point, at any rate, the Scripture speaks clearly and unmistakably.

The six verses of the passages before us are striking on many accounts. They are striking, if we consider the *event which* they describe: here is one Apostle rebuking another! – They are striking, when we consider who the two *men* are: Paul, the younger, rebukes Peter the elder! – They are striking, when we remark the *occasion*: this was no glaring fault, no flagrant sin, at first sight, that Peter had committed! Yet the Apostle Paul says, 'I withstood him to the face, because he was to be blamed.' He does more than this: – he reproves Peter publicly for his error before all the Church at Antioch. He goes even further: – he writes an account of the matter, which is now read in two hundred languages all over the world.

It is my firm conviction that the Holy Ghost means us to take particular notice of this passage of Scripture. If Christianity had been an invention of man, these things would never have been recorded. An impostor, like Mahomet, would have hushed up the difference between two Apostles. The Spirit of truth has caused these verses to be written for our learning, and we shall do well to take heed to their contents.

There are three great lessons from Antioch, which I think we ought to learn from this passage.

I. The *first* lesson is, that *great ministers may make great mistakes.*

II. The *second* is, that *to keep the truth of Christ in His Church is even more important than to keep peace.*

[94]

III. The *third* is, that *there is no doctrine about which we ought to be so jealous as justification by faith without the deeds of the law.*

I. The first great lesson we learn from Antioch is, that *great ministers may make great mistakes.*

What clearer proof can we have than that which is set before us in this place? Peter, without doubt, was one of the greatest in the company of the Apostles. He was an old disciple. He was a disciple who had had peculiar advantages and privileges. He had been a constant companion of the Lord Jesus. He had heard the Lord preach, seen the Lord work miracles, enjoyed the benefit of the Lord's private teaching, been numbered among the Lord's intimate friends, and gone out and come in with Him all the time He ministered upon earth. He was the Apostle to whom the keys of the kingdom of heaven were given, and by whose hand those keys were first used. He was the first who opened the door of faith to the Jews, by preaching to them on the day of Pentecost. He was the first who opened the door of faith to the Gentiles, by going to the house of Cornelius, and receiving him into the Church. He was the first to rise up in the Council of the fifteenth of Acts, and say, 'Why tempt ye God, to put a yoke upon the neck of the disciples, which neither our fathers nor we were able to bear?' And yet here this very Peter, this same Apostle, plainly falls into a great mistake. The Apostle Paul tells us, 'I withstood him to the face.' He tells us 'that he was to be blamed.' He says 'he feared them of the circumcision.' He says of him and his companions, that 'they walked not uprightly according to the truth of the Gospel.' He speaks of their 'dissimulation.' He tells us that by this dissimulation even Barnabas, his old companion in missionary labours, 'was carried away.'

What a striking fact this is. This is Simon Peter! This is the third great error of his, which the Holy Ghost has thought fit to record! Once we find him trying to keep back our Lord, as far as he could, from the great work of the cross, and severely rebuked. Then we find him denying the Lord three times, and with an oath. Here again we find him endangering the leading truth of Christ's Gospel. Surely we may say, 'Lord, what is man?' The Church of Rome boasts that the Apostle Peter is her founder and first Bishop. Be it so: grant it for a moment. Let us only remember, that of all the Apostles there is not one, excepting, of course, Judas Iscariot, of whom we have so many proofs that he was a *fallible* man. Upon her own showing the Church of Rome was founded by the most fallible of the Apostles.*

But it is all meant to teach us that even the Apostles themselves, when not writing under the inspiration of the Holy Ghost, were at times liable to err. It is meant to teach us that the best men are weak and fallible so long as they are in the body. Unless the grace of God holds them up, any one of them may go astray at any time. It is very humbling, but it is very true. True Christians are converted, justified, and sanctified. They are living members of Christ, beloved children of God, and heirs of eternal life. They are elect,

* It is curious to observe the shifts to which some writers have been reduced, in order to explain away the plain meaning of the verses which head this paper. Some have maintained that Paul did not really rebuke Peter, but only feignedly, for show and appearance sake! Others have maintained that it was not Peter the Apostle who was rebuked, but another Peter, one of the seventy! Such interpretations need no remark. They are simply absurd. The truth is that the plain honest meaning of the verses strikes a heavy blow at the favourite Roman Catholic doctrine of the primacy and superiority of Peter over the rest of the Apostles.

chosen, called, and kept unto salvation. They have the Spirit. But they are *not infallible*.

Will not rank and dignity confer infallibility? No: they will not! It matters nothing what a man is called. He may be a Czar, an Emperor, a King, a Prince. He may be a Pope or a Cardinal, an Archbishop or a Bishop, a Dean or an Archdeacon, a Priest or Deacon. He is still a *fallible man*. Neither the crown, nor the diadem, nor the annointing oil, nor the mitre, nor the imposition of hands, can prevent a man making mistakes.

Will not numbers confer infallibility? No: they will not! You may gather together princes by the score, and bishops by the hundred; but, when gathered together, they are still liable to err. You may call them a council, or a synod, or an assembly, or a conference, or what you please. It matters nothing. Their conclusions are still the conclusions of *fallible men*. Their collective wisdom is still capable of making enormous mistakes. Well says the twenty-first Article of the Church of England, 'General councils may err, and sometimes have erred, even in things pertaining unto God.'

The example of the Apostle Peter at Antioch is one that does not stand alone. It is only a parallel of many a case that we find written for our learning in holy Scripture. Do we not remember Abraham, the father of the faithful, following the advice of Sarah, and taking Hagar for a wife? Do we not remember Aaron, the first high priest, listening to the children of Israel, and making a golden calf? Do we not remember Nathan the prophet telling David to build a temple? Do we not remember Solomon, the wisest of men, allowing his wives to build their high places? Do we not remember Asa, the good king of Judah, seeking not to the Lord, but to the physicians? Do we not remember Jehosaphat, the good king, going down to help wicked Ahab? Do we not remember Hezekiah, the good king, receiving the ambassadors of Babylon? Do we not remember Josiah, the last of Judah's good kings, going forth to fight with Pharaoh? Do we not remember James and John, wanting fire to come down from heaven? These things deserve to be remembered. They were not written without cause. They cry aloud, *No infallibility!*

And who does not see, when he reads the history of the Church of Christ, repeated proofs that the best of men can err? The early fathers were zealous according to their knowledge, and ready to die for Christ. But many of them countenanced monkery, and nearly all sowed the seeds of many superstitions. – The Reformers were honoured instruments in the hand of God for reviving the cause of truth on earth. Yet hardly one of them can be named who did not make some great mistake. Martin Luther held pertinaciously the doctrine of consubstantiation. Melancthon was often timid and undecided. Calvin permitted Servetus to be burned. Cranmer recanted and fell away for a time from his first faith. Jewell subscribed to Popish doctrines for fear of death. Hooper disturbed the Church of England by over scrupulosity about vestments. The Puritans, in after times, denounced toleration as Abaddon and Apollyon. Wesley and Toplady, last century, abused each other in most shameful language. Irving, in our own day, gave way to the delusion of speaking in unknown tongues. All these things speak with a loud voice. They all lift up a beacon to the Church of Christ. They all say, 'Cease ye from man;' – 'Call no man master;' – 'Call no man father upon earth;' – 'Let no man glory in man;' – 'He that glorieth, let him glory in the Lord.' They all cry, *No infallibility!*

The lesson is one that we all need. We are all naturally inclined to lean upon man whom we can see, rather than upon God whom we cannot see. We naturally love to lean upon the ministers of the visible Church, rather than upon the Lord Jesus Christ, the great Shepherd and Bishop and High Priest, who is invisible. We need to be continually warned and set upon our guard.

I see this tendency to lean on man everywhere. I know no branch of the Protestant Church of Christ which does not require to be cautioned upon the point. It is a snare, for example, to the English Episcopalian to make idols of Bishop Pearson and 'the Judicious Hooker.' It is a snare to the Scotch Presbyterian to pin his faith on John Knox, the Covenanters, and Dr. Chalmers. It is a snare to the Methodists in our day to worship the memory of John Wesley. It is a snare to the Independent to see no fault in any opinion of Owen and Doddridge. It is a snare to the Baptist to exaggerate the wisdom of Gill, and Fuller, and Robert Hall. All these are snares, and into these snares how many fall!

We all naturally love to have a pope of our own. We are far too ready to think, that because some great minister or some learned man says a thing, – or because our own minister, whom we love, says a thing, – it must be right, without examining whether it is in Scripture or not. Most men dislike the trouble of thinking for themselves. They like following a leader. They are like sheep, – when one goes over the gap all the rest follow. Here at Antioch even Barnabas was carried away. We can well fancy that good man saying, 'An old Apostle, like Peter, surely cannot be wrong. Following him, I cannot err.'

And now let us see what practical lessons we may learn from this part of our subject.

(*a*) For one thing, let us learn not to put implicit confidence in any man's opinion, merely *because he lived many hundred years ago*. Peter was a man who lived in the time of Christ Himself, and yet he could err.

There are many who talk much in the present day about 'the voice of the primitive Church.' They would have us believe that those who lived nearest the time of the Apostles, must of course know more about truth than we can. There is no foundation for any such opinion. It is a fact, that the most ancient writers in the Church of Christ are often at variance with one another. It is a fact that they often changed their own minds, and retracted their own former opinions. It is a fact that they often wrote foolish and weak things, and often showed great ignorance in their explanations of Scripture. It is vain to expect to find them free from mistakes. *Infallibility is not to be found in the early fathers, but in the Bible.*

(*b*) For another thing, let us learn not to put implicit confidence in any man's opinion, *merely because of his office as a minister*. Peter was one of the very chiefest Apostles, and yet he could err.

This is a point on which men have continually gone astray. It is the rock on which the early Church struck. Men soon took up the saying, 'Do nothing contrary to the mind of the Bishop.' But what are bishops, priests, and deacons? What are the best of ministers but men, – dust, ashes, and clay, – men of like passions with ourselves, men exposed to temptations, men liable to weaknesses and infirmities? What saith the Scripture, 'Who is Paul and who is Apollos, but ministers by whom ye believed, even as the Lord gave to every man?' (1 Cor. 3:5.)

Bishops have often driven the truth into the wilderness, and decreed that to be true which was false. The greatest errors have been begun by ministers. Hophni and Phinehas, the sons of the High-priest, made religion to be abhorred by the children of Israel. Annas and Caiaphas, though in the direct line of descent from Aaron, crucified the Lord. Arius, that great heresiarch, was a minister. It is absurd to suppose that ordained men cannot go wrong. We should follow them so far as they teach according to the Bible, but no further. We should believe them so long as they can say, 'Thus it is written,' – 'thus saith the Lord;' but further than this we are not to go. *Infallibility is not to be found in ordained men, but in the Bible.*

(c) For another thing, let us learn not to place implicit confidence in any man's opinion, *merely because of his learning.* Peter was a man who had miraculous gifts, and could speak with tongues, and yet he could err.

This is a point again on which many go wrong. This is the rock on which men struck in the middle ages. Men looked on Thomas Aquinas, and Duns Scotus, and Peter Lombard, and many of their companions, as almost inspired. They gave epithets to some of them in token of their admiration. They talked of 'the irrefragable' doctor, 'the seraphic' doctor, 'the incomparable' doctor, – and seemed to think that whatever these doctors said must be true! But what is the most learned of men, if he be not taught by the Holy Ghost? What is the most learned of all divines but a mere fallible child of Adam at his very best? Vast knowledge of books and great ignorance of God's truth may go side by side. They have done so, they may do so, and they will do so in all times. I will engage to say that the two volumes of Robert M'Cheyne's Memoirs and Sermons, have done more positive good to the souls of men, than any one folio that Origen or Cyprian ever wrote. I doubt not that the one volume of 'Pilgrim's Progress,' – written by a man who knew hardly any book but his Bible, and was ignorant of Greek and Latin, – will prove in the last day to have done more for the benefit of the world, than all the works of the schoolmen put together. Learning is a gift that ought not to be despised. It is an evil day when books are not valued in the Church. But it is amazing to observe how vast a man's intellectual attainments may be, and yet how little he may know of the grace of God. I have no doubt the Authorities of Oxford in the last century, knew more of Hebrew, Greek, and Latin, than Wesley, Whitefield, Berridge, or Venn. But they knew little of the Gospel of Christ. *Infallibility is not to be found among learned men, but in the Bible.*

(*d*) For another thing, let us take care that we do not place implicit confidence *on our own minister's opinion*, however godly he may be. Peter was a man of mighty grace, and yet he could err.

Your minister may be a man of God indeed, and worthy of all honour for his preaching and practice; but do not make a pope of him. Do not place his word side by side with the Word of God. Do not spoil him by flattery. Do not let him suppose he can make no mistakes. Do not lean your whole weight on his opinion, or you may find to your cost that he can err.

It is written of Joash, King of Judah, that he 'did that which was right in the sight of the Lord all the days of Jehoiada the priest.' (2 Chron. 24:2.) Jehoiada died, and then died the religion of Joash. Just so your minister may die, and then your religion may die too; – may change, and your religion may change; – may go away, and your religion may go. Oh, be not satisfied with a religion built upon man! Be not content with saying, 'I have hope, because my own minister has told me such and such things.' Seek to be able to say, 'I have hope, because I find it thus and thus written in the Word of God.' If your peace is to be solid, you must go yourself to the fountain of all truth. If your comforts are to be lasting, you must visit the well of life yourself, and draw fresh water for your own soul. Ministers may depart from the faith. The visible Church may be broken up. But he who has the Word of God written in his heart, has a foundation beneath his feet which will never fail him. Honour your minister as a faithful ambassador of Christ. Esteem him very highly in love for his work's sake. But never forget that *infallibility is not to be found in godly ministers, but in the Bible.*

The things I have mentioned are worth remembering. Let us bear them in mind, and we shall have learned one lesson from Antioch.

II. I now pass on to the second lesson that we learn from Antioch. That lesson is, *that to keep Gospel truth in the Church is of even greater importance than to keep peace.*

I suppose no man knew better the value of peace and unity than the Apostle Paul. He was the Apostle who wrote to the Corinthians about charity. He was the Apostle who said, 'Be of the same mind one toward another;' – 'Be at peace among yourselves;' – 'Mind the same things;' – 'The servant of God must not strive;' – 'There is one body and there is one Spirit, even as ye are called in one hope of your calling, one Lord, one faith, one baptism.' He was the Apostle who said, 'I become all things to all men, that by all means I may save some.' (Rom. 12:16; 1 Thess.

5 : 13; Phil. 3 : 16; Eph. 4 : 5; 1 Cor. 9 : 22.) Yet see how he acts here! He withstands Peter to the face. He publicly rebukes him. He runs the risk of all the consequences that might follow. He takes the chance of everything that might be said by the enemies of the Church at Antioch. Above all, he writes it down for a perpetual memorial, that it never might be forgotten, – that, wherever the Gospel is preached throughout the world, this public rebuke of an erring Apostle might be known and read of all men.

Now, why did he do this? Because he dreaded false doctrine, – because he knew that a little leaven leaveneth the whole lump, – because he would teach us that we ought to contend for the truth jealously, and to fear the loss of truth more than the loss of peace.

St. Paul's example is one we shall do well to remember in the present day. Many people will put up with anything in religion, if they may only have a quiet life. They have a morbid dread of what they call 'controversy.' They are filled with a morbid fear of what they style, in a vague way, 'party spirit,' though they never define clearly what party spirit is. They are possessed with a morbid desire to keep the peace, and make all things smooth and pleasant, even though it be at the expense of truth. So long as they have outward calm, smoothness, stillness, and order, they seem content to give up everything else. I believe they would have thought with Ahab that Elijah was a troubler of Israel, and would have helped the princes of Judah when they put Jeremiah in prison, to stop his mouth. I have no doubt that many of these men of whom I speak, would have thought that Paul at Antioch was a very imprudent man, and that he went too far!

I believe this is all wrong. We have no right to expect anything but the pure Gospel of Christ, unmixed and un-adulterated, – the same Gospel that was taught by the Apostles, – to do good to the souls of men. I believe that to maintain this pure truth in the Church men should be ready to make any sacrifice, to hazard peace, to risk dis-sension, and run the chance of division. *They should no more tolerate false doctrine than they would tolerate sin.* They should withstand any adding to or taking away from the simple message of the Gospel of Christ.

For the truth's sake, our Lord Jesus Christ denounced the Pharisees, though they sat in Moses' seat, and were the appointed and authorized teachers of men. 'Woe unto you, Scribes and Pharisees, hypocrites,' He says, eight times over, in the twenty-third chapter of Matthew. And who shall dare to breathe a suspicion that our Lord was wrong?

For the truth's sake, Paul withstood and blamed Peter, though a brother. Where was the use of unity when pure doctrine was gone? And who shall dare to say he was wrong?

For the truth's sake, Athanasius stood out against the world to maintain the pure doctrine about the divinity of Christ, and waged a controversy with the great majority of the professing Church. And who shall dare to say he was wrong?

For the truth's sake, Luther broke the unity of the Church in which he was born, denounced the Pope and all his ways, and laid the foundation of a new teaching. And who shall dare to say that Luther was wrong?

For the truth's sake, Cranmer, Ridley, and Latimer, the English Reformers, counselled Henry VIII. and Edward VI. to separate from Rome, and to risk the consequences of division. And who shall dare to say that they were wrong?

For the truth's sake, Whitefield and Wesley, a hundred years ago, denounced the mere barren moral preaching of the clergy of their day, and went out into the highways and byways to save souls, knowing well that they would be cast out from the Church's communion. And who shall dare to say that they were wrong?

Yes! peace without truth is a false peace; it is the very peace of the devil. Unity without the Gospel is a worthless unity; it is the very unity of hell. Let us never be ensnared by those who speak kindly of it. Let us remember the words of our Lord Jesus Christ: 'Think not that I came to send peace upon earth. I came not to send peace, but a sword.' (Matt. 10:34.) Let us remember the praise He gives to one of the Churches in the Revelation: 'Thou canst not bear them who are evil. Thou hast tried them which say they are Apostles, and are not, and hast found them liars.' (Rev. 2:2.) Let us remember the blame He casts upon another: 'Thou sufferest that woman Jezebel to teach.' (Rev. 2:20.) Never let us be guilty of sacrificing any portion of truth upon the altar of peace. Let us rather be like the Jews, who, if they found any manuscript copy of the Old Testament Scriptures incorrect in a single letter, burned the whole copy, rather than run the risk of losing one jot or tittle of the Word of God. Let us be content with nothing short of the whole Gospel of Christ.

In what way are we to make practical use of the general principles which I have just laid down? I will give my readers one simple piece of advice. I believe it is advice which deserves serious consideration.

I warn then every one who loves his soul, *to be very jealous as to the preaching he regularly hears, and the place of worship he regularly attends.* He who deliberately settles down under any ministry which is positively unsound is a very unwise man. I will never hesitate to speak my mind on this point. I kncw well that many think it a shocking thing for a man to forsake his parish church. I cannot see with the eyes of such people. I draw a wide distinction between teaching which is *defective* and teaching which is thoroughly *false*, – between teaching which errs on the negative side and teaching which is positively unscriptural. But I do believe, if false doctrine is unmistakably preached in a parish church, a parishioner who loves his soul is quite right in not going to that parish church. To hear unscriptural teaching fifty-two Sundays in every year is a serious thing. It is a continual dropping of slow poison into the mind. I think it almost impossible for a man wilfully to submit himself to it, and not take harm. I see in the New Testament we are plainly told to 'prove all things,' and 'hold fast that which is good.' (1 Thess. 5 : 21.) I see in the Book of Proverbs that we are commanded to 'cease to hear the instruction which causeth to err from the paths of knowledge.' (Prov. 19 : 27.) If these words do not justify a man in ceasing to worship at a church, if positively false doctrine is preached in it, I know not what words can.

Does any one mean to tell us that to attend the parish church is absolutely needful to an Englishman's salvation? * If there is such an one, let him speak out, and give us his name. – Does any one mean to tell us that going to the parish church will save any man's soul, if he dies un-

---

* The next few pages have immediate reference to a Church of England context. The principle Ryle expounds, however, may profitably be applied to Nonconformists, namely that denominational loyalty must never take precedence over loyalty to the truth. [*Publishers.*]

converted and ignorant of Christ? If there is such an one, let him speak out, and give us his name. – Does any one mean to tell us that going to the parish church will teach a man anything about Christ, or conversion, or faith, or repentance, if these subjects are hardly ever named in the parish church, and never properly explained? If there is such an one, let him speak out, and give us his name. – Does any one mean to say that a man who repents, believes in Christ, is converted and holy, will lose his soul, because he has forsaken his parish church and learned his religion elsewhere? If there is such an one, let him speak out, and give us his name. – For my part I abhor such monstrous and extravagant ideas. I see not a jot of foundation for them in the Word of God. I trust that the number of those who deliberately hold them is exceedingly small.

There are not a few parishes in England where the religious teaching is little better than Popery. Ought the laity of such parishes to sit still, be content, and take it quietly? They ought not. And why? Because, like St. Paul, they ought to prefer truth to peace.

There are not a few parishes in England where the religious teaching is little better than morality. The distinctive doctrines of Christianity are never clearly proclaimed. Plato, or Seneca, or Confucius, or Socinus, could have taught almost as much. Ought the laity in such parishes to sit still, be content, and take it quietly? They ought not. And why? Because, like St. Paul, they ought to prefer truth to peace.

I am using strong language in dealing with this part of my subject: I know it. – I am trenching on delicate ground: I know it. – I am handling matters which are generally let alone, and passed over in silence: I know it. – I say what I say from a sense of duty to the Church of which I am a minister. I believe the state of the times, and the position of the laity in some parts of England, require plain speaking. Souls are perishing, in many parishes, in ignorance. Honest members of the Church of England, in many districts, are disgusted and perplexed. This is no time for smooth words. I am not ignorant of those magic expressions, 'the parochial system, order, division, schism, unity, controversy,' and the like. I know the cramping, silencing influence which they seem to exercise on some minds. I too have considered those expressions calmly and deliberately, and on each of them I am prepared to speak my mind.

(*a*) The *parochial system* of England is an admirable thing in theory. Let it only be well administered, and worked by truly spiritual ministers, and it is calculated to confer the greatest blessings on the nation. But it is useless to expect attachment to the parish church, when the minister of the parish is ignorant of the Gospel or a lover of the world. In such a case we must never be surprised if men forsake their parish church, and seek truth wherever truth is to be found. If the parochial minister does not preach the Gospel and live the Gospel, the conditions on which he claims the attention of his parishioners are *virtually violated*, and his claim to be heard is at an end. It is absurd to expect the head of a family to endanger the souls of his children, as well as his own, for the sake of 'parochial order.' There is no mention of parishes in the Bible, and we have no right to require men to live and die in ignorance, in order that they may be able to say at last, 'I always attended my parish church.'

(*b*) *Divisions and separations* are most objectionable in religion. They weaken the cause of true Christianity. They give occasion to the enemies of all godliness to blas-

[109]

pheme. But before we blame people for them, we must be careful that we lay the blame *where it is deserved*. False doctrine and heresy are even worse than schism. If people separate themselves from teaching which is positively false and unscriptural, they ought to be praised rather than reproved. In such cases separation is a virtue and not a sin. It is easy to make sneering remarks about 'itching ears,' and 'love of excitement;' but it is not so easy to convince a plain reader of the Bible that it is his duty to hear false doctrine every Sunday, when by a little exertion he can hear truth. The old saying must never be forgotten, 'He is the schismatic who causes the schism.'

(c) *Unity, quiet, and order* among professing Christians are mighty blessings. They give strength, beauty, and efficiency to the cause of Christ. But even gold may be bought too dear. Unity which is obtained by the sacrifice of truth is worth nothing. It is not the unity which pleases God. The Church of Rome boasts loudly of a unity which does not deserve the name. It is unity which is obtained by taking away the Bible from the people, by gagging private judgment, by encouraging ignorance, by forbidding men to think for themselves. Like the exterminating warriors of old, the Church of Rome 'makes a solitude and calls it peace.' There is quiet and stillness enough in the grave, but it is not the quiet of health, but of death. It was the false prophets who cried 'Peace,' when there was no peace.

(d) *Controversy* in religion is a hateful thing. It is hard enough to fight the devil, the world and the flesh, without private differences in our own camp. But there is one thing which is even worse than controversy, and that is false doctrine tolerated, allowed, and permitted without protest or molestation. It was controversy that won the battle of Protestant Reformation. If the views that some men hold were correct, it is plain we never ought to have had any Reformation at all! For the sake of peace, we ought to have gone on worshipping the Virgin, and bowing down to images and relics to this very day! Away with such trifling! There are times when controversy is not only a duty but a benefit. Give me the mighty thunderstorm rather than the pestilential malaria. The one walks in darkness and poisons us in silence, and we are never safe. The other frightens and alarms for a little season. But it is soon over, and it clears the air. It is a plain Scriptural duty to 'contend earnestly for the faith once delivered to the saints.' (Jude 3.)

I am quite aware that the things I have said are exceedingly distasteful to many minds. I believe many are content with teaching which is not the whole truth, and fancy it will be 'all the same' in the end. I am sorry for them. I am convinced that nothing but *the whole truth* is likely, as a general rule, to do good to souls. I am satisfied that those who wilfully put up with anything short of the whole truth, will find at last that their souls have received much damage. Three things there are which men never ought to trifle with, – a little poison, a little false doctrine, and a little sin.

I am quite aware that when a man expresses such opinions as those I have just brought forward, there are many ready to say, 'He is no Churchman.' I hear such accusations unmoved. The day of judgment will show who were the true friends of the Church of England and who were not. I have learned in the last thirty-two years that if a clergyman leads a quiet life, lets alone the unconverted part of the world, and preaches so as to offend none and edify none, he will be called by many 'a good Churchman.' And I have also learned that if a man studies the Articles and Homilies, labours continually for the conversion of souls, adheres closely to the great principles of the Reformation, bears a faithful testimony against Popery, and preaches as Jewell and Latimer used to preach, he will probably be thought a firebrand and 'troubler of Israel,' and called no Churchman at all! But I can see plainly that they are not the best Churchmen who talk most loudly about Churchmanship. I remember that none cried 'Treason' so loudly as Athaliah. (2 Kings 11 : 14.) Yet she was a traitor herself. I have observed that many who once talked most about Churchmanship have ended by forsaking the Church of England, and going over to Rome. Let men say what they will. *They are the truest friends of the Church of England who labour most for the preservation of truth.*

I lay these things before the readers of this paper, and invite their serious attention to them. I charge them never to forget that truth is of more importance to a Church than peace. I ask them to be ready to carry out the principles I have laid down, and to contend zealously, if needs be, for the truth. If we do this, we shall have learned something from Antioch.

III. But I pass on to the third lesson from Antioch. That lesson is, that *there is no doctrine about which we ought to be so jealous as justification by faith without the deeds of the law.*

The proof of this lesson stands out most prominently in the passage of Scripture which heads this paper. What one article of the faith had the Apostle Peter denied at Antioch? None. – What doctrine had he publicly preached which was false? None. – What, then, had he done? He had done this. After once keeping company with the believing Gentiles as 'fellow-heirs and partakers of the promise of Christ in the Gospel' (Eph. 3 : 6), he suddenly became shy of them and withdrew himself. He seemed to think they were less holy and acceptable to God than the circumcised Jews. He seemed to imply, that the believing Gentiles were in a lower state than they who had kept the ceremonies of the law of Moses. He seemed, in a word, to add something to simple *faith* as needful to give man an interest in Jesus Christ. He seemed to reply to the question, 'What shall I do to be saved?' not merely 'Believe on the Lord Jesus Christ,' but 'Believe on the Lord Jesus Christ, *and be circumcised*, and keep the ceremonies of the law.'

Such conduct as this the Apostle Paul would not endure for a moment. Nothing so moved him as the idea of adding anything to the Gospel of Christ. 'I withstood him,' he says, 'to the face.' He not only rebuked him, but he recorded the whole transaction fully, when by inspiration of the Spirit he wrote the Epistle to the Galatians.

I invite special attention to this point. I ask men to observe the remarkable jealousy which the Apostle Paul shows about this doctrine, and to consider the point about which such a stir was made. Let us mark in this passage of Scripture the immense importance of justification by faith without the deeds of the law. Let us learn here what mighty reasons the Reformers of the Church of England had for calling it, in our eleventh Article, 'a most wholesome doctrine and very full of comfort.'

(*a*) This is the doctrine which is *essentially necessary to our own personal comfort*. No man on earth is a real child of God, and a saved soul, till he sees and receives salvation by faith in Christ Jesus. No man will ever have solid peace and true assurance, until he embraces with all his heart the doctrine that 'we are accounted righteous before God for the merit of our Lord Jesus Christ, by faith, and not for our own works and deservings.' One reason, I believe, why so many professors in this day are tossed to and fro, enjoy little comfort, and feel little peace, is their ignorance on this point. They do not see clearly justification by faith without the deeds of the law.

(b) This is the doctrine which *the great enemy of souls hates, and labours to overthrow*. He knows that it turned the world upside down at the first beginning of the Gospel, in the days of the Apostles. He knows that it turned the world upside down again at the time of the Reformation. He is therefore always tempting men to reject it. He is always trying to seduce Churches and ministers to deny or obscure its truth. No wonder that the Council of Trent directed its chief attack against this doctrine, and pronounced it accursed and heretical. No wonder that many who think themselves learned in these days denounce the doctrine as theological jargon, and say that all 'earnest-minded people' are justified by Christ, whether they have faith or not! The plain truth is that the doctrine is all gall and wormwood to unconverted hearts. It just meets the wants of the awakened soul. But the proud unhumbled man who knows not his own sin, and sees not his own weakness, cannot receive its truth.

(c) This is the doctrine, the *absence of which accounts for half the errors of the Roman Catholic Church*. The beginning of half the unscriptural doctrines of Popery may be traced up to rejection of justification by faith. No Romish teacher, if he is faithful to his Church, can say to an anxious sinner, 'Believe on the Lord Jesus Christ and thou shalt be saved.' He cannot do it without additions and explanations, which completely destroy the good news. He dare not give the Gospel medicine, without adding something which destroys its efficacy, and neutralizes its power.

Purgatory, penance, priestly absolution, the intercession of saints, the worship of the Virgin, and many other man-made services of popery, all spring from this source. They are all rotten props to support weary consciences. But they are rendered necessary by the denial of justification by faith.

(*d*) This is the doctrine which is *absolutely essential to a minister's success among his people*. Obscurity on this point spoils all. Absence of clear statements about justification will prevent the utmost zeal doing good. There may be much that is pleasing and nice in a minister's sermons, much about Christ and sacramental union with Him, – much about self-denial, – much about humility, – much about charity. But all this will profit little, if his trumpet gives an uncertain sound about justification by faith without the deeds of the law.

(*e*) This is the doctrine which is *absolutely essential to the prosperity of a Church*. No Church is really in a healthy state, in which this doctrine is not prominently brought forward. A Church may have good forms and regularly ordained ministers. and the Sacraments properly administered, but a Church will not see conversion of souls going on under its pulpits, when this doctrine is not plainly preached. Its schools may be found in every parish. Its ecclesiastical buildings may strike the eye all over the land. But there will be no blessing from God on that Church, unless justification by faith is proclaimed from its pulpits. Sooner or later its candlestick will be taken away.

Why have the Churches of Africa and the East fallen to their present state? – Had they not bishops? They had. – Had they not forms and liturgies? They had. – Had they not synods and councils? They had. – But they cast away the doctrine of justification by faith. They lost sight of that mighty truth, and so they fell.

Why did our own Church do so little in the last century, and why did the Independents, and Methodists, and Baptists do so much more? – Was it that their system was better than ours? No. – Was it that our Church was not so well adapted to meet the wants of lost souls? No. – But their ministers preached justification by faith, and our ministers, in too many cases, did not preach the doctrine at all.

Why do so many English people go to dissenting chapels in the present day? Why do we so often see a splendid Gothic parish church as empty of worshippers as a barn in July, and a little plain brick building, called a Meeting House, filled to suffocation? Is it that people in general have any abstract dislike to Episcopacy, the Prayer-book, the surplice, and the establishment? Not at all! The simple reason is, in the vast majority of cases, that people do not like preaching in which justification by faith is not fully proclaimed. When they cannot hear it in the parish church they will seek it elsewhere. No doubt there are exceptions. No doubt there are places where a long course of neglect has thoroughly disgusted people with the Church of England, so that they will not even hear truth from its ministers. But I believe, as a general rule, when the parish church is empty and the meeting-house full, it will be found on inquiry that *there is a cause*.

If these things be so, the Apostle Paul might well be jealous for the truth, and withstand Peter to the face. He might well maintain that anything ought to be sacrificed, rather than endanger the doctrine of justification in the Church of Christ. He saw with a prophetical eye coming things. He left us all an example that we should do well to follow. Whatever we tolerate, let us never allow any injury to be done to that blessed doctrine, – that we are justified by faith without the deeds of the law.

Let us always beware of any teaching which either directly or indirectly obscures justification by faith. All religious systems which put anything between the heavy-laden sinner and Jesus Christ the Saviour, except simple faith, are dangerous and unscriptural. All systems which make out faith to be anything complicated, anything but a simple, childlike dependence, – the hand which receives the soul's medicine from the physician, – are unsafe and poisonous systems. All systems which cast discredit on the simple Protestant doctrine which broke the power of Rome, carry about with them a plague-spot, and are dangerous to souls.

Baptism is a sacrament ordained by Christ Himself, and to be used with reverence and respect by all professing Christians. When it is used rightly, worthily and with faith, it is capable of being the instrument of mighty blessings to the soul. But when people are taught that *all* who are baptized are as a matter of course born again, and that *all* baptized persons should be addressed as 'children of God,' I believe their souls are in great danger. Such teaching about baptism appears to me to overthrow the doctrine of justification by faith. They only are children of God who have faith in Christ Jesus. And all men have not faith.

The Lord's Supper is a sacrament ordained by Christ Himself, and intended for the edification and refreshment of true believers. But when people are taught that all persons ought to come to the Lord's table, whether they have faith or not; and that all alike receive Christ's body and blood who receive the bread and wine, I believe their souls are in great danger. Such teaching appears to me to darken the doctrine of justification by faith. No man eats Christ's body and drinks Christ's blood except the justified man. And none are justified until they believe.

Membership of the Church of England is a great privilege. No visible Church on earth, in my opinion, offers so many advantages to its members, when rightly administered. But when people are taught that because they are members of the Church, they are as a matter of course members of Christ, I believe their souls are in great danger. Such teaching appears to me to overthrow the doctrine of justification by faith. They only are joined to Christ who believe. And all men do not believe.

Whenever we hear teaching which obscures or contradicts justification by faith, we may be sure there is a screw loose somewhere. We should watch against such teaching, and be upon our guard. Once let a man get wrong about justification, and he will bid a long farewell to comfort, to peace, to lively hope, to anything like assurance in his Christianity. An error here is a worm at the root.

(1) In conclusion, let me first of all ask every one who reads this paper, to arm himself with a thorough *knowledge of the written Word of God*. Unless we do this we are at the mercy of any false teacher. We shall not see through the mistakes of an erring Peter. We shall not be able to imitate the faithfulness of a courageous Paul. An ignorant laity will always be the bane of a Church. A Bible-reading laity may save a Church from ruin. Let us read the Bible regularly, daily, and with fervent prayer, and become familiar with its contents. Let us receive nothing, believe nothing, follow nothing, which is not in the Bible, nor can be proved by the Bible. Let our rule of faith, our touchstone of all teaching, be the written Word of God.

(2) In the next place, let me recommend every member of the Church of England to make himself acquainted with *the Thirty-nine Articles of his own Church*. They are to be found at the end of most Prayer-books. They will abundantly repay an attentive reading. They are the true standard by which Churchmanship is to be tried, next to the Bible. They are the test by which Churchmen should prove the teaching of their ministers, if they want to know whether it is 'Church teaching' or not. I deeply lament the ignorance of systematic Christianity which prevails among many who attend the services of the Church of England. It would be well if such books as Archbishop Usher's 'Body of Divinity' were more known and studied than they are. If Dean Nowell's Catechism had ever been formally accredited as a formulary of the Church of England, many of the heresies of the last twenty years could never have lived for a day.* But unhappily many persons really know no more about the true doctrines of their own communion, than the heathen or Mahometans. It is useless to expect the laity of the Church of England to be zealous for the maintenance of true doctrine, unless they know what their own Church has defined true doctrine to be.

(3) In the next place, let me entreat all who read this paper to be always *ready to contend for the faith of Christ*, if needful. I recommend no one to foster a controversial spirit. I want no man to be like Goliath, going up and down, saying, 'Give me a man to fight with.' Always feeding upon controversy is poor work indeed. It is like feeding upon bones. But I do say that no love of false peace should

---

* Dean Nowell was Prolocutor of the Convocation which drew up the Thirty-nine Articles in the form in which we now have them, in the year 1562. His Catechism was approved and allowed by Convocation.

prevent us striving jealously against false doctrine, and seeking to promote true doctrine wherever we possibly can. True Gospel in the pulpit, true Gospel in every Religious Society we support, true Gospel in the books we read, true Gospel in the friends we keep company with, – let this be our aim, and never let us be ashamed to let men see that it is so.

(4) In the next place, let me entreat all who read this paper *to keep a jealous watch over their own hearts* in these controversial times. There is much need of this caution. In the heat of the battle we are apt to forget our own inner man. Victory in argument is not always victory over the world or victory over the devil. Let the meekness of St. Peter in taking a reproof, be as much our example as the boldness of St. Paul in reproving. Happy is the Christian who can call the person who rebukes him faithfully, a 'beloved brother.' (2 Peter 3 : 15.) Let us strive to be holy in all manner of conversation, and not least in our tempers. Let us labour to maintain an uninterrupted communion with the Father and with the Son, and to keep up constant habits of private prayer and Bible-reading. Thus we shall be armed for the battle of life, and have the sword of the Spirit well fitted to our hand when the day of temptation comes.

(5) In the last place, let me entreat all members of the Church of England who know what real praying is, *to pray daily for the Church to which they belong.* Let us pray that the Holy Spirit may be poured out upon it, and that its candlestick may not be taken away. Let us pray for those parishes in which the Gospel is now not preached, that the darkness may pass away, and the true light shine in them. Let us pray for those ministers who now neither know nor preach the truth, that God may take away the

veil from their hearts, and show them a more excellent way. Nothing is impossible. The Apostle Paul was once a persecuting Pharisee; Luther was once an unenlightened monk; Bishop Latimer was once a bigoted Papist; Thomas Scott was once thoroughly opposed to evangelical truth. Nothing, I repeat, is impossible. The Spirit can make clergymen preach that Gospel which they now labour to destroy. Let us therefore be instant in prayer.

I commend the matters contained in this paper to serious attention. Let us ponder them well in our hearts. Let us carry them out in our daily practice. Let us do this, and we shall have learned something from the story of St. Peter at Antioch.

7: Apostolic Fears

'I fear, lest by any means, as the serpent beguiled Eve by his subtilty, so your minds should be corrupted from the simplicity that is in Christ' (2 Cor. 11:3).

THE TEXT WHICH HEADS THIS PAGE, CONTAINS one part of the experience of a very famous Christian. No servant of Christ perhaps has left such a mark for good on the world as the Apostle St. Paul. When he was born the whole Roman Empire, excepting one little corner, was sunk in the darkest heathenism; when he died the mighty fabric of heathenism was shaken to its very centre, and ready to fall. And none of the agents whom God used to produce this marvellous change did more than Saul of Tarsus, after his conversion. Yet even in the midst of his successes and usefulness we find him crying out, 'I fear.'

There is a melancholy ring about these words which demands our attention. They show a man of many cares and anxieties. He who supposes that St. Paul lived a life of ease, because he was a chosen Apostle, wrought miracles, founded Churches, and wrote inspired Epistles, has yet much to learn. Nothing can be more unlike the truth! The eleventh chapter of the second Epistle to the Corinthians tells a very different tale. It is a chapter which deserves attentive study. Partly from the opposition of the heathen philosophers and priests, whose craft was in danger, – partly from the bitter enmity of his own unbelieving countrymen, – partly from false or weak brethren, – partly from his own thorn in the flesh, – the great Apostle of the Gentiles was like his Master, – 'a man of sorrows and acquainted with grief.' (Isa. 53:3.)

But of all the burdens which St. Paul had to carry, none seems to have weighed him down so much as that to which he refers, when he writes to the Corinthians, – 'the care of all the Churches.' (2 Cor. 11 : 28.) The scanty knowledge of many primitive Christians, – their weak faith, – their shallow experience, – their dim hope, – their low standard of holiness, – all these things made them peculiarly liable to be led astray by false teachers, and to depart from the faith. Like little children, hardly able to walk, they required to be treated with immense patience. Like exotics in a hothouse, they had to be watched with incessant care. Can we doubt that they kept their Apostolic founder in a state of constant tender anxiety? Can we wonder that he says to the Colossians, 'What great conflict I have for you'? – and to the Galatians, 'I marvel that ye are so soon removed from Him who called you into the grace of Christ unto another Gospel.' – 'O foolish Galatians, who hath bewitched you?' (Col. 2 : 1; Gal. 1 : 6; 3 : 1.) No attentive reader can study the Epistles without seeing this subject repeatedly cropping up. And the text I have placed at the head of this paper is a sample of what I mean : – 'I fear, lest by any means, as the serpent beguiled Eve by his subtilty, so your minds should be corrupted from the simplicity that is in Christ.' That text contains three important lessons, which I wish to press on the attention of all my readers. I believe in my conscience they are lessons for the times.

I. First, the text shows us a spiritual *disease to which we are all liable, and which we ought to fear*. That disease is corruption of our minds : – 'I fear lest your minds be corrupted.'

II. Secondly, the text shows us an *example which we*

ought to remember, as a beacon: – 'The serpent beguiled Eve by his subtilty.'

III. Thirdly, the text shows us *a point about which we ought specially to be on our guard.* That point is corruption 'from the simplicity that is in Christ.'

The text is a deep mine, and is not without difficulty. But let us go down into it boldly, and we shall find it contains much precious metal.

I. First, then, there is *a spiritual disease, which we ought to fear:* 'Corruption of mind.'

I take 'Corruption of mind' to mean injury of our minds by the reception of false and un-Scriptural doctrines in religion. And I believe the sense of the Apostle to be, 'I fear lest your minds should imbibe erroneous and unsound views of Christianity. I fear lest you should take up, as truths, principles which are not the truth. I fear lest you should depart from the faith once delivered to the saints, and embrace views which are practically destructive of the Gospel of Christ.'

The fear expressed by the Apostle is painfully instructive, and at first sight may create surprise. Who would have thought that under the very eyes of Christ's own chosen disciples, – while the blood of Calvary was hardly yet dry, while the age of miracles had not yet passed away, – who would have thought that in a day like this there was any danger of Christians departing from the faith? Yet nothing is more certain than that 'the mystery of iniquity' began already to work before the Apostles were dead. (2 Thess. 2:7.) 'Even now,' says St. John, 'There are many antichrists.' (1 John 2:18.) And no fact in Church history is more clearly proved than this – that false doctrine has never ceased to be the plague of Christendom for the last eighteen centuries. Looking forward with the eye of a prophet, St. Paul might well say 'I fear:' – 'I fear not merely the corruption of your morals, but of your minds.'

The plain truth is that *false doctrine* has been the chosen engine which Satan has employed in every age to stop the progress of the Gospel of Christ. Finding himself unable to prevent the Fountain of Life being opened, he has laboured incessantly to poison the streams which flow from it. If he could not destroy it, he has too often neutralized its usefulness by addition, subtraction, or substitution. In a word he has 'corrupted men's minds.'

(*a*) False doctrine soon overspread the Primitive Church after the death of the Apostles, whatever some may please to say of primitive purity. Partly by strange teaching about the Trinity and the Person of Christ, partly by an absurd multiplication of new-fangled ceremonies, partly by the introduction of monasticism and a man-made asceticism, the light of the Church was soon dimmed and its usefulness destroyed. Even in Augustine's time, as the preface to the English Prayer-book tells us, 'Ceremonies were grown to such a number that the estate of Christian people was in worse case concerning this matter than were the Jews.' Here was the corruption of men's minds.

(*b*) False doctrine in the middle ages so completely overspread the Church, that the truth as it is in Jesus was well nigh buried or drowned. During the last three centuries before the Reformation, it is probable that very few Christians in Europe could have answered the question, 'What must I do to be saved?' Popes and Cardinals, Abbots and Priors, Archbishops and Bishops, Priests and Deacons, Monks and Nuns, were, with a few rare exceptions, steeped in ignorance and superstition. They were sunk into a deep sleep, from which they were only partially roused by the earthquake of the Reformation. Here, again, was the 'corruption of men's minds.'

(c) False doctrine, since the days of the Reformation, has continually been rising up again, and marring the work which the Reformers began. Neologianism in some districts of Europe, Socinianism in others, formalism and indifferentism in others, have withered blossoms which once promised to bear good fruit, and made Protestantism a mere barren form. Here, again, has been the 'corruption of the mind.'

(d) False doctrine, even in our own day and under our own eyes, is eating out the heart of the Church of England and perilling her existence. One school of Churchmen does not hesitate to avow its dislike to the principles of the Reformation, and compasses sea and land to Romanize the Establishment. – Another school, with equal boldness, speaks lightly of inspiration, sneers at the very idea of a supernatural religion, and tries hard to cast overboard miracles as so much lumber. – Another school proclaims liberty to every shade and form of religious opinion, and tells us that all teachers are equally deserving our confidence, however heterogeneous and contradictory their opinions, if they are only clever, earnest, and sincere. To each and all the same remark applies. They illustrate the 'corruption of men's minds.'

In the face of such facts as these, we may well lay to heart the words of the Apostle in the text which heads the paper. Like him we have abundant cause to feel afraid. Never, I think, was there such need for English Christians to stand on their guard. Never was there such need for faithful ministers to cry aloud and spare not. 'If the trumpet give an uncertain sound, who shall prepare himself for the battle?' (1 Cor. 14 : 8.)

I charge every loyal member of the Church of England to open his eyes to the peril in which his own Church stands, and to beware lest it takes damage through apathy and a morbid love of peace. Controversy is an odious thing; but there are days when it is a positive duty. Peace is an excellent thing; but, like gold, it may be bought too dear. Unity is a mighty blessing; but it is worthless if it is purchased at the cost of truth. Once more I say, Open your eyes and be on your guard.

The nation that rests satisfied with its commercial prosperity, and neglects its national defences, because they are troublesome or expensive, is likely to become a prey to the first Alaric, or Attila, or Tamerlane, or Napoleon, who chooses to attack it. The Church which is 'rich, and increased with goods,' may think it has 'need of nothing,' because of its antiquity, orders, and endowments. It may cry 'Peace, peace,' and flatter itself it shall see no evil. But if it is not careful about the maintenance of sound doctrine among its ministers and members, it must never be surprised if its candlestick is taken away.

I deprecate, from the bottom of my heart, despondency or cowardice at this crisis. All I say is, let us exercise a godly fear. I do not see the slightest necessity for forsaking the old ship, and giving it up for lost. Bad as things look inside our ark, they are not a whit better outside. But I do protest against that careless spirit of slumber which seems to seal the eyes of many Churchmen, and to blind them to the enormous peril in which we are placed by the rise and progress of false doctrine in these days. I protest against the common notion so often proclaimed by men in high places, that *unity* is of more importance than sound doctrine, and *peace* more valuable than truth. And I call on every reader who really loves the Church of England to recognise the dangers of the times, and to do his duty, manfully and energetically, in resisting them by united action and by prayer. It was not for nothing that our Lord said, 'He that hath no sword, let him sell his garment and buy one.' (Luke 22:36.) Let us not forget St. Paul's words, 'Watch ye: stand fast in the faith. Quit you like men: be strong.' (1 Cor. 16:13.) Our noble Reformers bought the truth at the price of their own blood, and handed it down to us. Let us take heed that we do not basely sell it for a mess of pottage, under the specious names of unity and peace.

II. Secondly, the text shows us an *example we shall do well to remember, as a beacon:* 'The serpent beguiled Eve by his subtilty.'

I need hardly remind my readers that St. Paul in this place refers to the story of the fall in the third chapter of Genesis, as a simple historical fact. He does not afford the least countenance to the modern notion that the book of Genesis is nothing more than a pleasing collection of myths and fables. He does not hint that there is no such being as the devil, and that there was not any literal eating of the forbidden fruit, and that it was not really in this way that sin entered into the world. On the contrary, he narrates the story of the third of Genesis as a veracious history of a thing that really took place.

You should remember, moreover, that this reference does not stand alone. It is a noteworthy fact that several of the most remarkable histories and miracles of the Pentateuch are expressly mentioned in the New Testament, and always as historical facts. Cain and Abel, Noah's ark, the destruction of Sodom, Esau's selling his birthright, the destruction of the first-born in Egypt, the passage of the Red Sea, the brazen serpent, the manna, the water flowing from the rock, Balaam's ass speaking, – all these things are named by the writers of the New Testament, and named as matters of fact and not as fables. Let that never be forgotten. Those who are fond of pouring contempt on Old Testament miracles, and making light of the authority of the Pentateuch, would do well to consider whether they know better than our Lord Jesus Christ and the Apostles. To my mind, to talk of Genesis as a collection of myths and fables, in the face of such a text of Scripture as we have before us in this paper, sounds alike unreasonable and profane. Was St. Paul mistaken or not, when he narrated the story of the temptation and the fall? If he was, he was a weak-minded credulous person, and may have been mistaken on fifty other subjects. At this rate there is an end of all his authority as a writer! From such a monstrous conclusion we may well turn away with scorn. But it is well to remember that much infidelity begins with irreverent contempt of the Old Testament.

The point, after all, which the Apostle would have us mark in the history of Eve's fall, is the 'subtilty' with which the devil led her into sin. He did not tell her flatly that he wished to deceive her and do her harm. On the contrary, he told her that the thing forbidden was a thing that was 'good for food, and pleasant to the eyes, and to be desired to make one wise.' (Gen. 3:6.) He did not scruple to assert that she might eat the forbidden fruit and yet 'not die.' He blinded her eyes to the sinfulness and danger of transgression. He persuaded her to believe that to depart from God's plain command was for her benefit and not for her ruin. In short, 'he beguiled her by his subtilty.'

Now this 'subtilty,' St. Paul tells us, is precisely what we have to fear in false doctrine. We are not to expect it to approach our minds in the garment of error, but in the form of truth. Bad coin would never obtain currency if it had not some likeness to good. The wolf would seldom get into the fold if he did not enter it in sheep's clothing. Popery and infidelity would do little harm if they went about the world under their true names. Satan is far too wise a general to manage a campaign in such a fashion as this. He employs fine words and high-sounding phrases, such as 'Catholicity, Apostolicity, Unity, Church order, sound Church views, free thought, broad sense, kindly judgment, liberal interpretation of Scripture,' and the like, and thus effects a lodgment in unwary minds. And this is precisely the 'subtilty' which St. Paul refers to in the text. We need not doubt that he had read his Master's solemn words in the Sermon on the mount: 'Beware of false prophets, which come to you in sheep's clothing but inwardly they are ravening wolves.' (Matt 7:15.)

I ask your special attention to this point. Such is the simplicity and innocence of many Churchmen in this day, that they actually expect false doctrine to look false, and will not understand that the very essence of its mischievousness, as a rule, is its resemblance to God's truth. A young Churchman, for instance, brought up from his cradle to hear nothing but Evangelical teaching, is suddenly invited some day to hear a sermon preached by some eminent teacher of semi-Romish, or semi-sceptical opinions. He goes into the church, expecting in his simplicity to hear nothing but *heresy* from the beginning to the end. To his amazement he hears a clever, eloquent sermon, containing a vast amount of truth, and only a few homeopathic drops of error. Too often a violent reaction takes place in his simple, innocent, unsuspicious mind. He begins to think his former teachers were illiberal, narrow, and uncharitable, and his confidence in them is shaken, perhaps for ever. Too often, alas! it ends with his entire perversion, and at last he is enrolled in the ranks of the Ritualists or the Broad Churchmen! And what is the history of the whole case? Why, a foolish forgetfulness of the lesson St. Paul puts forward in this text. 'As the serpent beguiled Eve by his subtilty,' so Satan beguiles unwary souls in the nineteenth century by approaching them under the garb of truth.

I beseech every reader of this paper to remember this part of my subject, and to stand upon his guard. What more common than to hear it said of some false teacher in this day, – 'He is so good, so devoted, so kind, so zealous, so laborious, so humble, so self-denying, so charitable, so earnest, so fervent, so clever, so evidently sincere, there can be no danger and no harm in hearing him. Besides he preaches so much real Gospel: no one can preach a better sermon than he does sometimes! I never can and never will believe he is unsound.' – Who does not hear continually such talk as this? What discerning eye can fail to see that many Churchmen expect unsound teachers to be open vendors of poison, and cannot realize that they often appear as 'angels of light,' and are far too wise to be always saying all they think, and showing their whole hand and mind. But so it is. Never was it so needful to remember the words, 'The serpent beguiled Eve by his subtilty.'

I leave this part of my subject with the sorrowful remark that we have fallen upon times when *suspicion* on the subject of sound doctrine is not only a duty but a virtue. It is not the avowed Pharisee and Sadducee that we have to fear, but the *leaven* of the Pharisees and Sadducees.

It is the 'show of wisdom' with which Ritualism is invested that makes it so dangerous to many minds. (Col. 2:23.) It seems so good, and fair, and zealous, and holy, and reverential, and devout, and kind, that it carries away many well-meaning people like a flood. He that would be safe must cultivate the spirit of a sentinel at a critical post. He must not mind being laughed at and ridiculed, as one who 'has a keen nose for heresey.' In days like these he must not be ashamed to *suspect* danger. And if any one scoffs at him for so doing, he may well be content to reply, 'The serpent beguiled Eve by his subtilty.'

III. The third and last lesson of the text remains yet to be considered. It shows us *a point about which we ought to be especially on our guard*. That point is called 'The simplicity that is in Christ.'

Now the expression before us is somewhat remarkable, and stands alone in the New Testament. One thing at any rate is abundantly clear: the word *simplicity* means that which is single and unmixed, in contradistinction to that which is mixed and double. Following out that idea, some have held that the expression means 'singleness of affection towards Christ;' – we are to fear lest we should divide our affections between Christ and any other. This is no doubt very good theology; but I question whether it is the true sense of the text. – I prefer the opinion that the expression means the simple, unmixed, unadulterated, unaltered doctrine of Christ, – the simple 'truth as it is in Jesus,' on all points, – without addition, subtraction, or substitution. Departure from the simple genuine prescription of the Gospel, either by leaving out any part or adding any part, was the thing St. Paul would have the Corinthians specially dread. The expression is full of meaning, and seems specially written for our learning in these last days. We are to be ever jealously on our guard, lest we depart from and corrupt the *simple* Gospel which Christ once delivered to the saints.

The expression before us is exceedingly instructive. The principle it contains is of unspeakable importance. If we love our souls and would keep them in a healthy state, we must endeavour to adhere closely to the *simple doctrine of Christ*, in every jot, tittle, and particular. Once add to it or take away anything from it, and you risk spoiling the Divine medicine, and may even turn it into poison. Let your ruling principle be, – 'No other doctrine but that of Christ; nothing less, and nothing more!' Lay firm hold on that principle, and never let it go. Write it on the table of your heart, and never forget it.

(1) Let us settle it, for example, firmly in our minds, that there is *no way of peace* but the simple way marked out by Christ. True rest of conscience and inward peace of soul will never come from anything but direct faith in Christ Himself and His finished work. Peace by auricular confession, or bodily asceticism, or incessant attendance at Church services, or frequent reception of the Lord's Supper, is a delusion and a snare. It is only by coming straight to Jesus Himself, labouring and heavy laden, and by believing, trusting communion with Him, that souls find rest. In this matter let us stand fast in 'the simplicity that is in Christ.'

(2) Let us settle it next in our minds that there is *no other priest* who can be in any way a mediator between yourself and God but Jesus Christ. He Himself has said, and His word shall not pass away, 'No man cometh unto the Father but by Me.' (John 14:6.) No sinful child of

Adam, whatever be his orders, and however high his ecclesiastical title, can ever occupy Christ's place, or do what Christ alone is appointed to do. The priesthood is Christ's peculiar office, and it is one which He has never deputed to another. In this matter also let us stand fast in 'the simplicity that is in Christ.'

(3) Let us settle it next in our minds that there is *no sacrifice for sin* except the one sacrifice of Christ upon the cross. Listen not for a moment to those who tell you that there is any sacrifice in the Lord's Supper, any repetition of Christ's offering on the cross, or any oblation of His body and blood, under the form of consecrated bread and wine. The one sacrifice for sins which Christ offered was a perfect and complete sacrifice, and it is nothing short of blasphemy to attempt to repeat it. 'By one offering He has perfected for ever them that are sanctified.' (Heb. 10:14.) In this matter also let us stand fast in the 'simplicity that is in Christ.'

(4) Let us settle it next in our minds that there is *no other rule of faith*, and judge of controversies, but that simple one to which Christ always referred, – the written Word of God. Let no man disturb our souls by such vague expressions as 'the voice of the Church, primitive antiquity, the judgment of the early Fathers,' and the like tall talk. Let our only standard of truth be the Bible, God's Word written. 'What saith the Scripture?' – 'What is written?' – 'How readest thou?' – 'To the law and the testimony!' – 'Search the Scriptures.' (Rom. 4:3; Luke 10:26; Isa. 8:20; John 5:39.) In this matter also let us stand fast in the 'simplicity that is in Christ.'

(5) Let us settle it next in our minds that there are *no other means of grace* in the Church which have any binding authority, except those well known and simple ones

which Christ and the Apostles have sanctioned. Let us regard with a jealous suspicion all ceremonies and forms of man's invention, when they are invested with such exaggerated importance as to thrust into the background God's own appointments. It is the invariable tendency of man's inventions to supersede God's ordinances. Let us beware of making the Word of God of none effect by human devices. In this matter also let us stand fast in the 'simplicity that is in Christ.'

(6) Let us settle it next in our minds that *no teaching about the Sacraments* is sound which gives them a power of which Christ says nothing. Let us beware of admitting that either baptism or the Lord's Supper can confer grace '*ex opere operato,*' – that is by their mere outward administration, independently of the state of heart of those who receive them. Let us remember that the only proof that baptized people and communicants have grace, is the exhibition of grace in their lives. The fruits of the Spirit are the only evidences that we are born of the Spirit and one with Christ, and not the mere reception of the Sacraments. In this matter also let us stand fast in the 'simplicity that is in Christ.'

(7) Let us settle it next in our minds that *no teaching about the Holy Ghost* is safe which cannot be reconciled with the simple teaching of Christ. They are not to be heard who assert that the Holy Ghost actually dwells in all baptized people, without exception, by virtue of their baptism, and that this grace within such people only needs to be 'stirred up.' The simple teaching of our Lord is, that He dwells only in those who are His believing disciples, and that the world neither knows, nor sees, nor can receive the Holy Spirit. (John 14 : 17.) His in-dwelling is the special

[135]

privilege of Christ's people, and where He is He will be seen. On this point also let us stand fast in the 'simplicity that is in Christ.'

(8) Finally let us settle it in our minds that no teaching can be thoroughly sound, in which truth is not set forth in *the proportion of Christ and the Apostles*. Let us beware of any teaching in which the main thing is an incessant exaltation of the Church, the ministry, or the sacraments, while such grand verities as repentance, faith, conversion, holiness, are comparatively left in a subordinate and inferior place. Place such teaching side by side with the teaching of the Gospels, Acts, and Epistles. Count up texts. Make a calculation. Mark how little *comparatively* is said in the New Testament about baptism, the Lord's Supper, the Church, and the ministry; and then judge for yourself what is the proportion of truth. In this matter also, I say once more, let us stand fast in the 'simplicity that is in Christ.'

The simple doctrine and rule of Christ, then – nothing added, nothing taken away, nothing substituted – this is the mark at which we ought to aim. This is the point from which departure ought to be dreaded. Can we improve on His teaching? Are we wiser than He? Can we suppose that He left anything of real vital importance unwritten, or liable to the vague reports of human traditions? Shall we take on ourselves to say that we can mend or change for the better any ordinance of His appointment? Can we doubt that in matters about which He is silent we have need to act very cautiously, very gently, very moderately, and must beware of pressing them on those who do not see with our eyes? Above all must we not beware of asserting anything to be needful to salvation of which Christ has said nothing at all? I only see one answer to such questions as these. We must beware of anything which has even the appearance of departure from the 'simplicity that is in Christ.'

The plain truth is that we cannot sufficiently exalt the Lord Jesus Christ as the great Head of the Church, and Lord of all ordinances, no less than as the Saviour of sinners. I take it we all fail here. We do not realize how high and great and glorious a King the Son of God is, and what undivided loyalty we owe to One who has not deputed any of His offices, or given His glory to another. The solemn words which John Owen addressed to the House of Commons, in a sermon on the 'Greatness of Christ,' deserve to be remembered. I fear the House of Commons hears few such sermons in the present day.

'Christ is the *way:* men without Him are Cains, wanderers, vagabonds. His is the *truth:* men without Him are liars, like the devil of old. He is the *life:* men without Him are dead in trespasses and sins. He is the *light:* men without Him are in darkness, and go they know not whither. He is the *vine:* men that are not in Him are withered branches prepared for the fire. He is the *rock:* men not built on Him are carried away with a flood. He is the *Alpha and Omega,* the first and the last, the author and the ender, the founder and finisher of our salvation. He that hath not Him hath neither beginning of good nor shall have end of misery. Oh, blessed Jesus, how much better were it not to be than to be without Thee! never to be born than not to die in Thee! A thousand hells come short of this, eternally to want Jesus Christ.' This witness is true. If we can say Amen to the spirit of this passage it will be well with our souls.

And now let me conclude this paper by offering a few

parting words of counsel to any one into whose hands it may fall. I offer them not as one who has any authority but one who is affectionately desirous to do good to his brethren. I offer them especially to all who are members of the Church of England, though I believe they will be found useful by all English Christians. And I offer them as counsels which I find helpful to my own soul, and as such I venture to think they will be helpful to others.

(1) In the first place, if we would be kept from falling away into false doctrine, *let us arm our minds with a thorough knowledge of God's Word*. Let us read our Bibles from beginning to end with daily diligence, and constant prayer for the teaching of the Holy Spirit, and so strive to become thoroughly familiar with their contents. Ignorance of the Bible is the root of all error, and a superficial acquaintance with it accounts for many of the sad perversions and defections of the present day. In a hurrying age of railways and telegraphs, I am firmly persuaded that many Christians do not give time enough to private reading of the Scriptures. I doubt seriously whether English people did not know their Bibles better two hundred years ago than they do now. The consequence is, that they are 'tossed to and fro, and carried about with every wind of doctrine,' and fall an easy prey to the first clever teacher of error who tries to influence their minds. I entreat my readers to remember this counsel, and take heed to their ways. It is as true now as ever, that the good *textuary* is the only good theologian, and that a familiarity with great leading texts, is, as our Lord proved in the temptation, one of the best safeguards against error. Arm yourself then with the sword of the Spirit, and let your hand become used to it. I am well aware that there is no

royal road to Bible-knowledge. Without diligence and pains no one ever becomes 'mighty in the Scriptures.' 'Justification,' said Charles Simeon, with his characteristic quaintness, 'is by faith, but knowledge of the Bible comes by works.' But of one thing I am certain: there is no labour which will be so richly repaid as laborious regular daily study of God's Word.

(2) In the second place, if we could keep a straight path, as Churchmen, in this evil day, *let us be thoroughly acquainted with the Thirty-nine Articles of the Church of England*. Those Articles, I am bold to say, are the authorised Confession of the Church of England, and the true test by which the teaching of every clergyman ought to be tried. The 'teaching of the Prayer-book' is a common phrase in many mouths, and the Prayer-book is often held up as a better standard of Churchmanship than the Articles. But I venture to assert that the Articles, and not the Prayer-book, are the Church's standard of Church doctrine. Let no one suppose that I think lightly of the Prayer-book, because I say this. In loyal love to the Liturgy, and deep admiration of its contents, I give place to no man. Taken for all in all, it is an incomparable book of devotion for the use of a Christian congregation. But the Church's Prayer-book was never meant to be the Church's fixed standard of Bible doctrine, in the same way that the Articles are. This was not meant to be its office: this was not the purpose for which it was compiled. It is a manual of devotion; it is not a confession of faith. Let us value it highly; but let us not exalt it to the place which the Articles alone can fill, and which common sense, statute law, and the express opinion of eminent divines agree in assigning to them.

I entreat every reader of this paper to search the Articles, and to keep up familiar acquaintance with them by reading them carefully at least once a year. Settle it in your mind that no man has a right to call himself a sound Churchman who preaches, teaches, or maintains anything contrary to the Church's confession of faith. I believe the Articles in this day are unduly neglected. I think it would be well if in all middle-class schools connected with the Church of England, they formed a part of the regular system of religious instruction. Like the famous Westminster Confession in Scotland, they would be found a mighty barrier against the tendency to return to Rome.

(3) The third and last counsel which I venture to offer is this. *Let us make ourselves thoroughly acquainted with the history of the English Reformation.* My reason for offering this counsel is my firm conviction that this highly important part of English history has of late years been undeservedly neglected. Thousands of Churchmen now-a-days have a most inadequate notion of the amount of our debt to our martyred Reformers. They have no distinct conception of the state of darkness and superstition in which our fathers lived, and of the light and liberty which the Reformation brought in. And the consequence is that they see no great harm in the Romanizing movement of the present day, and have very indistinct ideas of the real nature and work of Popery. It is high time that a better state of things should begin. Of one thing I am thoroughly convinced: a vast amount of the prevailing apathy about the Romanizing movement of the day may be traced up to gross ignorance, both of the true nature of Popery and of the Protestant Reformation.

Ignorance, after all, is one of the best friends of false doctrine. More light is one of the great wants of the day, even in the nineteenth century. Thousands are led astray by Popery or infidelity from sheer want of reading and information. Once more I repeat, if men would only study with attention the Bible, the Articles, and the History of the Reformation, I should have little fear of their 'minds being corrupted from the simplicity that is in Christ.' They might not, perhaps, be 'converted' to God, but at any rate they would not be 'perverted' from the Church of England.

8: Idolatry

'Flee from idolatry' (1 Cor. 10:14).

THE TEXT WHICH HEADS THIS PAGE MAY SEEM AT first sight to be hardly needed in England. In an age of education and intelligence like this, we might almost fancy it is waste of time to tell an Englishman to 'flee from idolatry.'

I am bold to say that this is a great mistake. I believe that we have come to a time when the subject of idolatry demands a thorough and searching investigation. I believe that idolatry is near us, and about us, and in the midst of us, to a very fearful extent. The second commandment, in one word, is in peril. 'The plague is begun.'

Without further preface, I propose in this paper to consider the four following points: –

I. *The definition of idolatry.* WHAT IS IT?

II. *The cause of idolatry.* WHENCE COMES IT?

III. *The form idolatry assumes in the visible Church of Christ.* WHERE IS IT?

IV. *The ultimate abolition of idolatry.* WHAT WILL END IT?

I feel that the subject is encompassed with many difficulties. Our lot is cast in an age when truth is constantly in danger of being sacrificed to toleration, charity, and peace, falsely so called. Nevertheless, I cannot forget, as a clergyman, that the Church of England is a Church which has 'given no uncertain sound' on the subject of idolatry; and, unless I am greatly mistaken, truth about idolatry is, in the highest sense, truth for the times.

I. Let me, then, first of all supply *a definition of idolatry*. Let me show WHAT IT IS.

It is of the utmost importance that we should understand this. Unless I make this clear, I can do nothing with the subject. Vagueness and indistinctness prevail upon this point, as upon almost every other in religion. The Christian who would not be continually running aground in his spiritual voyage, must have his channel well buoyed, and his mind well stored with clear definitions.

I say then, that '*idolatry is a worship in which the honour due to God in Trinity, and to Him only, is given to some of His creatures, or to some invention of His creatures.*' It may vary exceedingly. It may assume exceedingly different forms, according to the ignorance or the knowledge – the civilization or the barbarism, of those who offer it. It may be grossly absurd and ludicrous, or it may closely border on truth, and admit of being most speciously defended. But whether in the adoration of the idol of Juggernaut, or in the adoration of the host in St. Peter's at Rome, the principle of idolatry is in reality the same. In either case the honour due to God is turned aside from Him, and bestowed on that which is not God. And whenever this is done, whether in heathen temples or in professedly Christian Churches, there is an act of *idolatry*.

It is not necessary for a man formally to deny God and Christ, in order to be an idolater. Far from it. Professed reverence for the God of the Bible and actual idolatry, are perfectly compatible. They have often gone side by side, and they still do so. The children of Israel never thought of renouncing God when they persuaded Aaron to make the golden calf. 'These be thy gods,' they said (thy Elohim), 'which brought thee up out of the land of Egypt.' And the feast in honour of the calf was kept as 'a feast unto the Lord.' (Jehovah.) (Exod. 32:4, 5.) Jeroboam, again, never pretended to ask the ten tribes to cast off their allegiance to the God of David and Solomon. When he set up the calves of gold in Dan and Bethel, he only said, 'It is too much for you to go up to Jerusalem: behold thy gods, O Israel (thy Elohim), which brought thee up out of the land of Egypt.' (1 Kings 12:28.) In both instances, we should observe, the idol was not set up as a rival to God, but under the pretence of being a help – a stepping-stone to His service. But, in both instances, a great sin was committed. The honour due to God was given to a visible representation of Him. The majesty of Jehovah was offended. The second commandment was broken. There was, in the eyes of God, a flagrant act of *idolatry*.

Let us mark this well. It is high time to dismiss from our minds those loose ideas about idolatry, which are common in this day. We must not think, as many do, that there are only two sorts of idolatry, – the spiritual idolatry of the man who loves his wife, or child, or money more than God; and the open, gross idolatry of the man who bows down to an image of wood, or metal, or stone, because he knows no better. We may rest assured that idolatry is a sin which occupies a far wider field than this. It is not merely a thing in Hindostan, that we may hear of and pity at missionary meetings; nor yet is it a thing confined to our own hearts, that we may confess before the mercy-seat upon our knees. It is a pestilence that walks in the Church of Christ to a much greater extent than many suppose. It is an evil that, like the man of sin, 'sits in the very temple of God.' (2 Thess. 2:4.) It is a sin that we all need to watch and pray against continually. It creeps into our religious worship insensibly, and is upon us before we are aware. Those are tremendous words which Isaiah spoke to the formal Jew, – not to the worshipper of Baal, remember, but to the man who actually came to the temple (Isa. 66:3): 'He that killeth an ox is as if he slew a man; he that sacrificeth a lamb, as if he cut off a dog's neck; he that offereth an oblation, as if he offered swine's blood; he that burneth incense, as if he blessed an idol.'

This is that sin which God has especially denounced in His Word. One commandment out of ten is devoted to the prohibition of it. Not one of all the ten contains such a solemn declaration of God's character, and of His judgments against the disobedient: –' I the Lord thy God am a jealous God, visiting the iniquity of the fathers upon the children unto the third and fourth generation of them that hate Me.' (Exod. 20:5.) Not one, perhaps, of all the ten is so emphatically repeated and amplified, and especially in the fourth chapter of the book of Deuteronomy.

This is the sin, of all others, to which the Jews seem to have been most inclined before the destruction of Solomon's temple. What is the history of Israel under their judges and kings but a melancholy record of repeated falling away into idolatry? Again and again we read of 'high places' and false gods. Again and again we read of captivities and chastisements on account of idolatry. Again and again we read of a return to the old sin. It seems as if the love of idols among the Jews was naturally bone of their bone and flesh of their flesh. The besetting sin of the Old Testament Church, in one word, was idolatry. In the face of the most elaborate ceremonial ordinances that God ever gave to His people, Israel was incessantly turning aside after idols, and worshipping the work of men's hands.

This is the sin, of all others, which has brought down the heaviest judgments on the visible Church. It brought on Israel the armies of Egypt, Assyria, and Babylon. It scattered the ten tribes, burned up Jerusalem, and carried Judah and Benjamin into captivity. It brought on the Eastern Churches, in later days, the overwhelming flood of the Saracenic invasion, and turned many a spiritual garden into a wilderness. The desolation which reigns where Cyprian and Augustine once preached, the living death in which the Churches of Asia Minor and Syria are buried, are all attributable to this sin. All testify to the same great truth which the Lord proclaims in Isaiah: 'My glory will I not give to another.' (Isa. 42:8.)

Let us gather up these things in our minds, and ponder them well. Idolatry is a subject which, in every Church of Christ that would keep herself pure, should be thoroughly examined, understood, and known. It is not for nothing that St. Paul lays down the stern command, 'Flee from idolatry.'

II. Let me show, in the second place, *the cause to which idolatry may be traced*. WHENCE COMES IT?

To the man who takes an extravagant and exalted view of human intellect and reason, idolatry may seem absurd. He fancies it too irrational for any but weak minds to be endangered by it.

To a mere superficial thinker about Christianity, the peril of idolatry may seem very small. Whatever commandments are broken, such a man will tell us, professing Christians are not very likely to transgress the second.

Now, both these persons betray a woeful ignorance of human nature. They do not see that there are secret roots of idolatry within us all. The prevalence of idolatry in all ages among the heathen must necessarily puzzle the one, – the warnings of Protestant ministers against idolatry in the Church must necessarily appear uncalled for to the other. Both are alike blind to its cause.

The cause of all idolatry is the natural corruption of man's heart. That great family disease, with which all the children of Adam are infected from their birth, shows itself in this, as it does in a thousand other ways. Out of the same fountain from which 'proceed evil thoughts, adulteries, fornications, murders, thefts, covetousness, wickedness, deceit,' and the like (Mark 7:21, 22), – out of that same fountain arise false views of God, and false views of the worship due to Him; and, therefore, when the Apostle Paul tells the Galatians (Gal. 5:20) what are the 'works of the flesh,' he places prominently among them 'idolatry.'

A religion of some kind man will have. God has not left Himself without a witness in us all, fallen as we are. Like old inscriptions hidden under mounds of rubbish, – like the almost-obliterated underwriting of Palimpsest manuscripts,* – even so there is a dim *something* engraven at the bottom of man's heart, however faint and half-erased, – a *something* which makes him feel he must have a religion and a worship of some kind. The proof of this

---

* 'Palimpsest' is the name given to ancient parchment manuscripts which have been twice written over, that is, the work of a comparatively modern writer has been written over or across the work of an older writer. Before the invention of cheap paper, the practice of so writing over an old manuscript was not uncommon. The object of the practice, of course, was to save expense. The misfortune was that the second writing was often far less valuable that the first.

is to be found in the history of voyages and travels in every part of the globe. The exceptions to the rule are so few, if indeed there are any, that they only confirm its truth. Man's worship in some dark corner of the earth may rise no higher than a vague fear of an evil spirit, and a desire to propitiate him; but a worship of some kind man will have.

But then comes in the effect of the fall. Ignorance of God, carnal and low conceptions of His nature and attributes, earthly and sensual notions of the service which is acceptable to Him, all characterize the religion of the natural man. There is a craving in his mind after something he can see, and feel, and touch in his Divinity. He would fain bring his God down to his own crawling level. He would make his religion a thing of sense and sight. He has no idea of the religion of heart, and faith, and spirit. In short, just as he is willing to live on God's earth, but, until renewed by grace, a fallen and degraded life, so he has no objection to worship after a fashion, but, until renewed by the Holy Ghost, it is always with a fallen worship. In one word, idolatry is a natural product of man's heart. It is a weed, which like the earth uncultivated, the heart is always ready to bring forth.

And now does it surprise us, when we read of the constantly recurring idolatries of the Old Testament Church, – of Peor, and Baal, and Moloch, and Chemosh, and Ashtaroth, – of high places and hill altars, and groves and images, – and this in the full light of the Mosaic ceremonial? Let us cease to be surprised. It can be accounted for. There is a cause.

Does it surprise us when we read in history how idolatry crept in by degrees into the Church of Christ, – how little by little it thrust out Gospel truth, until, in Canterbury, men offered more at the shrine of Thomas á Becket, than they did at that of the Virgin Mary, and more at that of the Virgin Mary, than at that of Christ? Let us cease to be surprised. It is all intelligible. There is a cause.

Does it surprise us when we hear of men going over from Protestant Churches to the Church of Rome, in the present day? Do we think it unaccountable, and feel as if we ourselves could never forsake a pure form of worship for one like that of the Pope? Let us cease to be surprised. There is a solution for the problem. There is a cause.

That cause is nothing else but the corruption of man's heart. There is a natural proneness and tendency in us all to give God a sensual, carnal worship, and not that which is commanded in His Word. We are ever ready, by reason of our sloth and unbelief, to devise visible helps and stepping-stones in our approaches to Him, and ultimately to give these inventions of our own the honour due to Him. In fact, idolatry is all natural, down-hill, easy, like the broad way. Spiritual worship is all of grace, all up-hill, and all against the grain. Any worship whatsoever is more pleasing to the natural heart, than worshipping God in the way which our Lord Christ describes, 'in spirit and in truth.' (John 4:23.)

I, for one, am not surprised at the quantity of idolatry existing, both in the world and in the visible Church. I believe it perfectly possible that we may yet live to see far more of it than some have ever dreamed of. It would never surprise me if some mighty personal Antichrist were to arise before the end, – mighty in intellect, mighty in talents for government, aye, and mighty, *perhaps*, in miraculous gifts too. It would never surprise me to see such an one as him setting up himself in opposition to Christ, and forming an Infidel conspiracy and combination against the Gospel.

I believe that many would rejoice to do him honour, who now glory in·saying, 'We will not have this Christ to reign over us.' I believe that many would make a god of him, and reverence him as an incarnation of truth, and concentrate their idea of hero-worship on his person. I advance it as a *possibility*, and no more. But of this at least I am certain, – that no man is less safe from danger of idolatry than the man who now sneers at every form of religion; and that from Infidelity to credulity, from Atheism to the grossest idolatry, there is but a single step. Let us not think, at all events, that idolatry is an old-fashioned sin, into which we are never likely to fall. 'Let him that thinketh he standeth, take heed lest he fall.' We shall do well to look into our own hearts: the seeds of idolatry are all there. We should remember the words of St. Paul. 'Flee from idolatry.'

III. Let me show, in the third place, *the forms which idolatry has assumed, and does assume in the visible Church.* WHERE IS IT?

I believe there never was a more baseless fabric than the theory which obtains favour with many, – that the promises of perpetuity and preservation from apostasy, belong to the visible Church of Christ. It is a theory supported neither by Scripture nor by facts. The Church against which 'the gates of hell shall never prevail,' is not the visible Church, but the whole body of the elect, the company of true believers out of every nation and people. The greater part of the visible Church has frequently maintained gross heresies. The particular branches of it are never secure against deadly error, both of faith and practice. A departure from the faith, – a falling away, – a leaving of first love in any branch of the visible Church, need never surprise a careful reader of the New Testament.

That idolatry would arise, seems to have been the expectation of the Apostles, even before the canon of the New Testament was closed. It is remarkable to observe how St. Paul dwells on this subject in his Epistle to the Corinthians. If any Corinthian called a brother was an idolater, with such an one the members of the Church 'were not to eat.' (1 Cor. 5:11.) 'Neither be ye idolaters, as were some of our fathers.' (1 Cor. 10:7.) He says again, in the text which heads this paper, 'My dearly beloved, flee from idolatry.' (1 Cor. 10:14.) When he writes to the Colossians, he warns them against 'worshipping of angels.' (Col. 2:18.) And St. John closes his first Epistle with the solemn injunction, 'Little children, keep yourselves from idols.' (1 John 5:21.) It is impossible not to feel that all these passages imply an expectation that idolatry would arise, and that soon, among professing Christians.

The famous prophecy in the fourth chapter of the first Epistle to Timothy contains a passage which is even more directly to the point: 'The Spirit speaketh expressly, that in the latter times some shall depart from the faith, giving heed to seducing spirits, and doctrines of devils.' (1 Tim. 4:1.) I will not detain my readers with any lengthy discussion of that remarkable expression, 'doctrines of devils.' It may be sufficient to say that our excellent translators of the Bible are considered for once to have missed the full meaning of the Apostle in their rendering of the word translated as 'devils' in our version, and that the true meaning of the expression is, 'doctrines about departed spirits.' And in this view, which, I may as well say, is maintained by all those who have the best right to be heard on such a question, the passage becomes a direct prediction of the rise of that most specious form of idolatry, the *worship of dead saints*. (See Mede's Works.)

The last passage I will call attention to, is the conclusion of the ninth chapter of Revelation. We there read, at the twentieth verse: 'The rest of the men which were not killed by these plagues, yet repented not of the works of their hands, that they should not worship devils' (this is the same word, we should observe, as that in the Epistle to Timothy, just quoted), 'and idols of gold, and silver, and brass, and stone, and wood: which neither can see, nor hear, nor walk.' Now, I am not going to offer any comment on the chapter in which this verse occurs. I know well there is a difference of opinion as to the true interpretation of the plagues predicted in it. I only venture to assert, that it is the highest probability these plagues are to fall upon the visible Church of Christ; and the highest improbability, that St. John was here prophesying about the heathen, who never heard the Gospel. And this once conceded, the fact that idolatry is *a predicted sin of the visible Church*, does seem most conclusively and for ever established.

And now, if we turn from the Bible to facts, what do we see? I reply unhesitatingly, that there is unmistakable proof that Scripture warnings and predictions were not spoken without cause, and that idolatry has actually arisen in the visible Church of Christ, and does still exist.

The rise and progress of the evil in former days, we shall find well summed up in the Homily of the Church of England, on Peril of Idolatry. To that Homily I beg to refer all churchmen, reminding them once for all, that in the judgment of the Thirty-nine Articles, the Book of Homilies 'contains a godly and wholesome doctrine, and necessary for these times.' – There we read, how, even in the FOURTH CENTURY, Jerome complains, 'that the errors

[152]

of images have come in, and passed to the Christians from the Gentiles;' and Eusebius says, 'We do see that images of Peter and Paul, and of our Saviour Himself be made, and tables be painted, which I think to have been derived and kept indifferently by an heathenish custom.'—There we may read, how 'Pontius Paulinus, Bishop of Nola, in the *fifth century*, caused the walls of the temples to be painted with stories taken out of the Old Testament; that the people beholding and considering these pictures might the better abstain from too much surfeiting and riot. But from learning by painted stories, it came by little and little to idolatry.' – There we may read how Gregory the first, Bishop of Rome, in the beginning of the *seventh century*, did allow the free having of images in churches. – There we may read how Irene, mother of Constantine the Sixth, in the *eighth century*, assembled a Council at Nicæa, and procured a decree that images should be put up in all the churches of Greece, and that honour and worship should be given to the said images.' And there we may read the conclusion with which the Homily winds up its historical summary, – 'that laity and clergy, learned and unlearned, all ages, sorts, and degrees of men, women and children of whole Christendom, have been at once drowned in abominable idolatry, of all other vices most detested by God, and most damnable to man, and that by the space of 800 years and more.'

This is a mournful account, but it is only too true. There can be little doubt the evil began even before the time just mentioned by the Homily writers. No man, I think, need wonder at the rise of idolatry in the Primitive Church who considers calmly the excessive reverence which it paid, from the very first, to the visible parts of religion. I believe that no impartial man can read the language used by nearly all the Fathers about the Church, the bishops, the ministry, baptism, the Lord's Supper, the martyrs, the dead saints generally, – no man can read it without being struck with the wide difference between their language and the language of Scripture on such subjects. You seem at once to be in a new atmosphere. You feel that you are no longer treading on holy ground. You find that things which in the Bible are evidently of second-rate importance, are here made of first-rate importance. You find the things of sense and sight exalted to a position in which Paul, and Peter, and James, and John, speaking by the Holy Ghost, never for a moment placed them. It is not merely the weakness of un-inspired writings that you have to complain of; it is something worse; it is a new system. And what is the explanation of all this? It is, in one word, that you have got into a region where the malaria of idolatry has begun to arise. You perceive the first workings of the mystery of iniquity. You detect the buds of that huge system of idol-atry which, as the Homily describes, was afterwards formally acknowledged, and ultimately blossomed so luxuriantly in every part of Christendom.

But let us now turn from the past to the present. Let us examine the question which most concerns ourselves. Let us consider in what form idolatry presents itself to us as a sin of the visible Church of Christ in our own time.

I find no difficulty in answering this question. I feel no hesitation in affirming that idolatry never yet assumed a more glaring form than it does *in the Church of Rome at this present day*.

And here I come to a subject on which it is hard to speak, because of the times we live in. But the whole truth ought to be spoken by ministers of Christ, without respect of times and prejudices. And I should not lie down in peace, after writing on idolatry, if I did not declare my solemn conviction that idolatry is one of the crying sins of which the Church of Rome is guilty. I say this in all sadness. I say it, acknowledging fully that we have our faults in the Protestant Church; and practically, perhaps, in some quarters, not a little idolatry. But from formal, recognised, systematic idolatry, I believe we are almost entirely free. While, as for the Church of Rome, if there is not in her worship an enormous quantity of systematic, organized idolatry, I frankly confess I do not know what idolatry is.

(*a*) To my mind, it is idolatry to have images and pictures of saints in churches, and to give them a reverence for which there is no warrant or precedent in Scripture. And if this be so, I say there *is idolatry in the Church of Rome*.

(*b*) To my mind, it is idolatry to invoke the Virgin Mary and the saints in glory, and to address them in language never addressed in Scripture except to the Holy Trinity. And if this be so, I say there is *idolatry in the Church of Rome*.

(*c*) To my mind, it is idolatry to bow down to mere material things, and attribute to them a power and sanctity far exceeding that attached to the ark or altar of the Old Testament dispensation; and a power and sanctity, too, for which there is not a tittle of foundation in the Word of God. And if this be so, with the holy coat of Treves, and the wonderfully-multiplied wood of the true cross, and a thousand other so-called relics in my mind's eye, I say there is *idolatry in the Church of Rome*.

(*d*) To my mind, it is idolatry to worship that which man's hands have made, – to call it God, and adore it when lifted up before our eyes. And if this be so, with the notorious doctrine of transubstantiantion, and the elevation of the host in my recollection, I say there is *idolatry in the Church of Rome*.

(*e*) To my mind, it is idolatry to make ordained men mediators between ourselves and God, robbing, as it were, our Lord Christ of His office, and giving them an honour which even Apostles and angels in Scripture flatly repudiate. And if this be so, with the honour paid to Popes and Priests before my eyes, I say there is *idolatry in the Church of Rome*.

I know well that language like this jars the minds of many. Men love to shut their eyes against evils which it is disagreeable to allow. They will not see things which involve unpleasant consequences. That the Church of Rome is an *erring* Church, they will acknowledge. That she is *idolatrous*, they will deny.

They tell us that the reverence which the Romish Church gives to saints and images does not amount to idolatry. They inform us that there are distinctions between the worship of 'latria' and 'dulia,' between a mediation of redemption, and a mediation of intercession, which clear her of the charge. My answer is, that the Bible knows nothing of such distinctions; and that, in the actual practice of the great bulk of Roman Catholics, they have no existence at all.*

They tell us, that it is a mistake to suppose that Roman Catholics really worship the images and pictures before which they perform acts of adoration; that they only use them as helps to devotion, and in reality look far beyond

---

* 'Latria' and 'dulia' are two Greek words, both meaning 'worship' or 'service,' but the former being a much stronger word than the latter. The Roman Catholic admits that the worship of 'latria' may not be given to saints, but maintains that 'dulia' may be given.

them. My answer is, that many a heathen could say just as much for his idolatry; – that it is notorious, in former days, they did say so; – and that in Hindostan many idol-worshippers do say so at the present day. But the apology does not avail. The terms of the second commandment are too stringent. It prohibits *bowing down*, as well as worshipping. And the very anxiety which the Church of Rome has often displayed to exclude that second commandment from her catechisms, is of itself a great fact which speaks volumes to a candid observer.

They tell us that we have no evidence for the assertions we make on this subject; that we found our charges on the abuses which prevail among the ignorant members of the Romish communion; and that it is absurd to say that a Church containing so many wise and learned men, is guilty of idolatry. My answer is, that the devotional books in common use among Roman Catholics supply us with unmistakable evidence. Let any one examine that notorious book, '*The Garden of the Soul*,' if he doubts my assertion, and read the language there addressed to the Virgin Mary. Let him remember that this language is addressed to a woman, who, though highly favoured, and the mother of our Lord, was yet one of our fellow-sinners, – to a woman, who actually confesses her need of a Saviour for herself. She says, 'My spirit hath rejoiced in God my Saviour.' (Luke 1:47.) Let him examine this language in the light of the New Testament, and then let him tell us fairly, whether the charge of idolatry is not fully made out. – But I answer, beside this, that we want no better evidence than that which is supplied in the city of Rome itself. What do men and women do under the light of the Pope's own countenance? What is the religion that prevails around St. Peter's and under the walls of the

Vatican? What is Romanism at Rome, unfettered, un-shackled, and free to develop itself in full perfection? Let a man honestly answer these questions, and I ask no more. Let him read such a book as Seymour's 'Pilgrimage to Rome,' or 'Alford's Letters,' and ask any visitor to Rome if the picture is too highly coloured. Let him do this, I say, and I believe he cannot avoid the conclusion, that Romanism in perfection is a gigantic system of Church-worship, Sacrament-worship, Mary-worship, saint-worship, image-worship, relic-worship, and priest-worship, – that it is, in one word, a *huge organized idolatry.*

I know how painful these things sound to many ears. To me it is no pleasure to dwell on the shortcomings of any who profess and call themselves Christians. I can say truly, that I have said what I have said with pain and sorrow.

I draw a wide distinction between the accredited dogmas of the Church of Rome and the private opinions of many of her members. I believe and hope that many a Roman Catholic is in heart inconsistent with his profession, and is better than the Church to which he belongs. I cannot forget the Jansenists, and Quesnel, and Martin Boos. I believe that many a poor Italian at this day is worshipping with an idolatrous worship, simply because he knows no better. He has no Bible to instruct him. He has no faithful minister to teach him. He has the fear of the priest before his eyes, if he dares to think for himself. He has no money to enable him to get away from the bondage he lives under, even if he feels a desire. I remember all this; and I say that the Italian eminently deserves our sympathy and compassion. But all this must not prevent my saying that the Church of Rome is an *idolatrous Church.*

I should not be faithful if I said less. The Church of

which I am a minister has spoken out most strongly on the subject. The Homily on Peril of Idolatry, and the solemn protest following the Rubrics, at the end of our Prayer-book Communion Service, which denounces the adoration of the Sacramental bread and wine as 'idolatry to be abhorred of all faithful Christians,' are plain evidence that I have said no more than the mind of my own Church. And in a day like this, – when some are disposed to secede to the Church of Rome, and many are shutting their eyes to her real character, and wanting us to be re-united to her, – in a day like this, my own conscience would rebuke me if I did not warn men plainly that the Church of Rome is an idolatrous Church, and that if they will join her they are '*joining themselves to idols.*'

But I may not dwell longer on this part of my subject. The main point I wish to impress on men's minds is this, – that idolatry has decidedly manifested itself in the visible Church of Christ, and nowhere so decidedly as in the Church of Rome.

IV. And now let me show, in the last place, the *ultimate abolition of all idolatry.* WHAT WILL END IT?

I consider that man's soul must be in an unhealthy state who does not long for the time when idolatry shall be no more. That heart can hardly be right with God which can think of the millions who are sunk in heathenism, or honour the false prophet Mahomet, or daily offer up prayers to the Virgin Mary, and not cry, 'O my God, what shall be the end of these things? How long, O Lord, how long?'

Here, as in other subjects, the sure word of prophecy comes in to our aid. The end of all idolatry shall one day come. Its doom is fixed. Its overthrow is certain. Whether in heathen temples, or in so-called Christian Churches, idolatry shall be destroyed at the second coming of our Lord Jesus Christ.

Then shall be fulfilled the prophecy of Isaiah, 'The idols He shall utterly abolish.' (Isa. 2:18.) – Then shall be fulfilled the words of Micah (5:13): 'Their graven images also will I cut off, and their standing images out of the midst of thee, and thou shalt no more worship the work of thine hands.' – Then shall be fulfilled the prophecy of Zephaniah (2:11): 'The Lord will be terrible unto them: for He will famish all the gods of the earth; and men shall worship Him, every one from his place, even all the isles of the heathen.' – Then shall be fulfilled the prophecy of Zechariah (13:2): 'It shall come to pass at that day, saith the Lord of hosts, that I will cut off the names of the idols out of the land, and they shall no more be remembered.' – In a word the 97th Psalm shall then receive its full accomplishment: 'The Lord reigneth: let the earth rejoice; let the multitude of isles be glad thereof. Clouds and darkness are round about Him: righteousness and judgment are the habitation of His throne. A fire goeth before Him, and burneth up His enemies round about. His lightnings enlightened the world: the earth saw, and trembled. The hills melted like wax at the presence of the Lord, at the presence of the Lord of the whole earth. The heavens declare His righteousness, and all the people see His glory. Confounded be all they that serve graven images, that boast themselves of idols: worship Him, all ye gods.'

The second coming of our Lord Jesus Christ is that blessed hope which should ever comfort the children of God under the present dispensation. It is the pole-star by which we must journey. It is the one point on which all our expectations should be concentrated. 'Yet a little while, and He that shall come will come, and will not tarry.' (Heb. 10:37.) Our David shall no longer dwell in Adullam, followed by a despised few, and rejected by the many. He shall take to Himself His great power, and reign, and cause every knee to bow before Him.

Till then our redemption is not perfectly enjoyed; as Paul tells the Ephesians, 'We are sealed unto the day of redemption.' (Eph. 4:30.) Till then our salvation is not completed; as Peter says, 'We are kept by the power of God through faith unto salvation ready to be revealed in the last time.' (1 Peter 1:5.) Till then our knowledge is still defective; as Paul tells the Corinthians: 'Now we see through a glass darkly; but then face to face: now I know in part; then shall I know even also as I am known.' (1 Cor. 13:12.) In short, our best things are yet to come.

But in the day of our Lord's return every desire shall receive its full accomplishment. We shall no more be pressed down and worn out with the sense of constant failure, feebleness, and disappointment. In His presence we shall find there is a *fulness* of joy, if nowhere else; and when we awake up after His likeness we shall be *satisfied*, if we never were before. (Psalm 16:11; 17:15.)

There are many abominations now in the visible Church, over which we can only sigh and cry, like the faithful in Ezekiel's day. (Ezek. 9:4.) We cannot remove them. The wheat and the tares will grow together until the harvest. But a day comes when the Lord Jesus shall once more purify His temple, and cast forth everything that defiles. He shall do that work of which the doing of Hezekiah and Josiah were a faint type long ago. He shall cast forth the images, and purge out idolatry in every shape.

Who is there now that longs for the conversion of the heathen world? You will not see it in its fulness until the

Lord's appearing. Then, and not till then, will that often-misapplied text be fulfilled: 'A man shall cast his idols of silver, and his idols of gold, which they made each one for himself to worship, to the moles and to the bats.' (Isa. 2:20.)

Who is there now that longs for the redemption of Israel? You will never see it in its perfection till the Redeemer comes to Zion. Idolatry in the professing Church of Christ has been one of the mightiest stumbling-blocks in the Jew's way. When it begins to fall, the veil over the heart of Israel shall begin to be taken away. (Psalm 102:16.)

Who is there now that longs for the fall of Anti-Christ, and the purification of the Church of Rome? I believe that will never be until the winding up of this dispensation. That vast system of idolatry may be consumed and *wasted* by the Spirit of the Lord's mouth, but it shall never be *destroyed* excepting by the brightness of His coming. (2 Thess. 2:8.)

Who is there now that longs for a perfect Church – a Church in which there shall not be the slightest taint of idolatry? You must wait for the Lord's return. Then, and not till then, shall we see a perfect Church, – a Church having neither spot nor wrinkle, nor any such thing (Eph. 5:27), – a Church of which all the members shall be regenerate, and every one a child of God.

If these things be so, men need not wonder that we urge on them the study of prophecy, and that we charge them above all to grasp firmly the glorious doctrine of Christ's second appearing and kingdom. This is the 'light shining in a dark place' to which we shall do well to take heed. Let others indulge their fancy if they will, with the vision of an imaginary 'Church of the future.' Let the children of this world dream of some 'coming man,' who is to understand everything, and set everything right. They are only sowing to themselves bitter disappointment. They will awake to find their visions baseless and empty as a dream. It is to such as these that the Prophet's words may be well applied: 'Behold, all ye that kindle a fire, that compass yourselves about with sparks: walk in the light of your fire, and in the sparks that ye have kindled. This shall ye have of Mine hand; ye shall lie down in sorrow.' (Isa. 50:11.)

But let your eyes look right onward to the day of Christ's second advent. That is the only day when every abuse shall be rectified, and every corruption and source of sorrow completely purged away. Waiting for that day, let us each work on and serve our generation; not idle, as if nothing could be done to check evil, but not disheartened because we see not yet all things put under our Lord. After all, the night is far spent, and the day is at hand. Let us wait, I say, on the Lord.

If these things be so, men need not wonder that we warn them to beware of all leanings towards the Church of Rome. Surely, when the mind of God about idolatry is so plainly revealed to us in His Word, it seems the height of infatuation in any one to join a Church so steeped in idolatries as the Church of Rome. To enter into communion with her, when God is saying, 'Come out of her, that ye be not partakers of her sins, and receive not of her plagues' (Rev. 18:4), – to seek her when the Lord is warning us to leave her, – to become her subjects when the Lord's voice is crying, 'Escape for thy life, flee from the wrath to come;' all this is mental blindness indeed, – a blindness like that of him, who, though forewarned, embarks in a sinking ship, – a blindness which would be

[163]

almost incredible, if our own eyes did not see examples of it continually.

We must all be on our guard. We must take nothing for granted. We must not hastily suppose that we are too wise to be ensnared, and say, like Hazael, 'Is Thy servant a dog, that he should do this thing?' Those who preach must cry aloud and spare not, and allow no false tenderness to make them hold their peace about the heresies of the day. Those who hear must have their loins girt about with truth, and their minds stored with clear prophetical views of the end to which all idol-worshippers must come. Let us all try to realize that the latter ends of the world are upon us, and that the abolition of all idolatry is hastening on. Is this a time for a man to draw nearer to Rome? Is it not rather a time to draw further back and stand clear, lest we be involved in her downfall? Is this a time to extenuate and palliate Rome's manifold corruptions, and refuse to see the reality of her sins? Surely we ought rather to be doubly jealous of everything of a Romish tendency in religion, – doubly careful that we do not connive at any treason against our Lord Christ – and doubly ready to protest against unscriptural worship of every description. Once more, then, I say, let us remember that the destruction of all idolatry is certain, and remembering that, *beware of the Church of Rome.*

The subject I now touch upon is of deep and pressing importance, and demands the serious attention of all Protestant Churchmen. It is vain to deny that a large party of English clergy and laity in the present day are moving heaven and earth to reunite the Church of England with the idolatrous Church of Rome. The publication of that monstrous book, Dr. Pusey's 'Eirenicon', and the formation of a 'Society for Promoting the Union of Christendom,' are plain evidence of what I mean. He that runs may read.

The existence of such a movement as this will not surprise any one who has carefully watched the history of the Church of England during the last forty years. The tendency of Tractarianism and Ritualism has been steadily towards Rome. Hundreds of men and women have fairly and honestly left our ranks, and become downright Papists. But many hundreds more have stayed behind, and are yet nominal Churchmen within our pale. The pompous semi-Romish ceremonial which has been introduced into many churches, has prepared men's minds for changes. An extravagantly theatrical and idolatrous mode of celebrating the Lord's Supper has paved the way for transubstantiation. A regular process of *unprotestantizing* has been long and successfully at work. The poor old Church of England stands on an inclined plane. Her very existence, as a Protestant Church, is in peril.

I hold, for one, that this Romish movement ought to be steadily and firmly resisted. Notwithstanding the rank, the learning, and the devotedness of some of its advocates, I regard it as a most mischievous, soul-ruining and unscriptural movement. To say that re-union with Rome would be an insult to our martyred Reformers, is a very light thing; it is far more than this: it would be a sin and an offence against God! Rather than be re-united with the idolatrous Church of Rome, I would willingly see my own beloved Church perish and go to pieces. Rather than become Popish once more, she had better die!

Unity in the abstract is no doubt an excellent thing: but unity without truth is useless. Peace and uniformity are beautiful and valuable: but peace without the Gospel, – peace based on a common Episcopacy, and not on a common faith, – is a worthless peace, not deserving of the name. When Rome has repealed the decrees of Trent, and her additions to the Creed, – when Rome has recanted her false and unscriptural doctrines, – when Rome has formally renounced image-worship, Mary-worship, and transubstantiation, – then, and not till then, it will be time to talk of re-union with her. Till then there is a gulf between us which cannot be honestly bridged. Till then I call on all Churchmen to resist to the death this idea of re-union with Rome. Till then let our watch-words be 'No peace with Rome! No communion with idolaters!' Well says the admirable Bishop Jewell, in his Apology, 'We do not decline concord and peace with men; but we will not continue in a state of war with God that we might have peace with men! – If the Pope does indeed desire we should be reconciled to him, he ought first to reconcile himself to God.' This witness is true! Well would it be for the Church of England, if all her bishops had been like Jewell!

I write these things with sorrow. But the circumstances of the times make it absolutely necessary to speak out. To whatever quarter of the horizon I turn, I see grave reason for alarm. For the true Church of Christ I have no fears at all. But for the Established Church of England, and for all the Protestant Churches of Great Britain, I have very grave fears indeed. The tide of events seems running strongly against Protestantism and in favour of Rome. It looks as if God had a controversy with us, as a nation, and was about to punish us for our sins.

I am no prophet. I know not where we are drifting. But at the rate we are going, I think it quite within the verge of possibility that in a few years the Church of England may be reunited to the Church of Rome. The Crown of

England may be once more on the head of a Papist. Protestantism may be formally repudiated. A Romish Archbishop may once more preside at Lambeth Palace. Mass may be once more said at Westminster Abbey and St. Paul's. And one result will be that all Bible-reading Christians must either leave the Church of England, or else sanction idol-worship and become idolaters! God grant we may never come to this state of things! But at the rate we are going, it seems to me quite possible.

And now it only remains for me to conclude what I have been saying, by mentioning some safeguards for the souls of all who read this paper. We live in a time when the Church of Rome is walking amongst us with renewed strength, and loudly boasting that she will soon win back the ground that she has lost. False doctrines of every kind are continually set before us in the most subtle and specious forms. It cannot be thought unseasonable if I offer some practical safeguards against idolatry. What it is, whence it comes, where it is, what will end it, – all this we have seen. Let me point out how we may be safe from it, and I will say no more.

(1) Let us arm ourselves, then, for one thing, with *a thorough knowledge of the Word of God*. Let us read our Bibles more diligently than ever, and become familiar with every part of them. Let the Word dwell in us richly. Let us beware of anything which would make us give less time, and less heart, to the perusal of its sacred pages. The Bible is the sword of the Spirit; – let it never be laid aside. The Bible is the true lantern for a dark and cloudy time; – let us beware of travelling without its light. I strongly suspect, – if we did but know the secret history of the numerous secessions from our Church to that of Rome, which we

deplore, – I strongly suspect that in almost every case one of the most important steps in the downward road would be found to have been a neglected Bible, – more attention to forms, sacraments, daily services, primitive Christianity, and so forth, and diminished attention to the written Word of God. The Bible is the King's highway. If we once leave that for any by-path, however beautiful, and old, and frequented it may seem, we must never be surprised if we end with worshipping images and relics, and going regularly to a confessional.

(2) Let us arm ourselves, in the second place, with *a godly jealousy about the least portion of the Gospel*. Let us beware of sanctioning the slightest attempt to keep back any jot or tittle of it, or to throw any part of it into the shade by exalting subordinate matters in religion. When Peter withdrew himself from eating with the Gentiles, it seemed but a little thing; yet Paul tells the Galatians, 'I withstood him to the face, because he was to be blamed.' (Gal. 2 : 11.) Let us count nothing little that concerns our souls. Let us be very particular whom we hear, where we go, and what we do, in all the matters of our own particular worship, and let us care nothing for the imputation of squeamishness and excessive scrupulosity. We live in days when great principles are involved in little acts, and things in religion, which fifty years ago were utterly indifferent, are now by circumstances rendered indifferent no longer. Let us beware of tampering with anything of a Romanizing tendency. It is foolishness to play with fire. I believe that many of our perverts and seceders began with thinking there could be no mighty harm in attaching a *little* more importance to certain outward things than they once did. But once launched on the downward course, they went on from one thing to another. They provoked God,

and He left them to themselves! They were given over to strong delusion, and allowed to believe a lie. (2 Thess. 2:11.) They tempted the devil, and he came to them! They started with trifles, as many foolishly call them. They have ended with downright idolatry.

(3) Let us arm ourselves, last of all, with *clear, sound views of our Lord Jesus Christ*, and of the salvation that is in Him. He is the 'image of the invisible God,' – the express 'image of His person,' – and the true preservative against all idolatry, when truly known. Let us build ourselves deep down on the strong foundation of His finished work upon the cross. Let us settle it firmly in our minds, that Christ Jesus has done everything needful in order to present us without spot before the throne of God, and that simple, childlike faith on our part is the only thing required to give us an entire interest in the work of Christ. Let us not doubt that having this faith, we are completely justified in the sight of God, – will never be more justified if we live to the age of Methuselah and do the works of the Apostle Paul, – and CAN add nothing to that complete justification by any acts, deeds, words, performances, fastings, prayers, almsdeeds, attendance on ordinances, or anything else of our own.

Above all let us keep up continual communion with the person of the Lord Jesus! Let us abide in Him daily, feed on Him daily, look to Him daily, lean on Him daily, live upon Him daily, draw from His fulness daily. Let us realize this, and the idea of other mediators, other comforters, other intercessors, will seem utterly absurd. 'What need is there?' we shall reply: 'I have Christ, and in Him I have all. What have I to do with idols? I have Jesus in my heart, Jesus in the Bible, and Jesus in heaven, and I want nothing more!'

Once let the Lord Christ have His rightful place in our hearts, and all other things in our religion will soon fall into their right places. – Church, ministers, sacraments, ordinances, all will go down, and take the second place.

Except Christ sits as Priest and King upon the throne of our hearts, that little kingdom within will be in perpetual confusion. But only let Him be 'all in all' there, and all will be well. Before Him every idol, every Dagon shall fall down. CHRIST RIGHTLY KNOWN, CHRIST TRULY BELIEVED, AND CHRIST HEARTILY LOVED, IS THE TRUE PRESERVATIVE AGAINST RITUALISM, ROMANISM, AND EVERY FORM OF IDOLATRY.

NOTE.

I ask every reader of this paper to read, mark, learn, and inwardly digest the language of the following declaration. It is the declaration which, under the 'Act of Settlement' and by the law of England, every Sovereign of this country, at his or her coronation, must 'make, subscribe, and audibly repeat.' It is the declaration, be it remembered, which was made, subscribed and repeated by Her Gracious Majesty, Queen Victoria.

'I, Victoria, do solemnly and sincerely, in the presence of God, profess, testify, and declare that I do believe that in the Sacrament of the Lord's Supper there is not any transubstantiation of the elements of bread and wine into the body and blood of Christ, at or after the consecration thereof, by any person whatsoever; and that the invocation or adoration of the Virgin Mary or any other Saint, and the sacrifice of the mass, as they are now used in the Church of Rome, are superstitious, and *idolatrous.* And I do solemnly, in the presence of God, profess, testify, and declare, that I do make this declaration, and every part thereof, in the plain and ordinary sense of the words read unto me, as they are commonly understood by English Protestants, without any evasion, equivocation or mental reservation, and without any dispensation already granted me for this purpose by the Pope or any other authority or person whatsoever, or without any hope of any such dispensation from any person or authority whatsoever, or without thinking that I am or can be acquitted before God or man, or absolved of this declaration or any part thereof, although the Pope, or any other person or persons or power whatsoever, shall dispense with or annul the same, or declare that it was null and void from the beginning.'

May the day never come when British Sovereigns shall cease to make the above declaration!